Behavior Essentials, Visualized

A teacher's visual guide to supporting students with diverse needs

Acknowledgments

We would first like to thank our amazingly talented illustrator, Saliha, who has assisted us with making these behavioral strategies come to life. With her help, we were able to capture details and emotions in the drawings so that readers can quickly grasp the concepts and relate to each scenario. Saliha has been an integral part of ABA Visualized over the years, and we are so happy to have her talent shown within these pages.

We would also like to recognize our collaborators who generously offered their immeasurable expertise as educators, service providers, administrators, advocates, and neurodiverse self-advocates: Alex Baughns, Tamar Bedoyan, Camila Grullon, Carver McDonald, Chelsea Pierce, Maddie Fry, Kali Hayter, Kristen Morrison, Nadia Guajardo, Betsy Rushing, Leslie Sanders, Arielle Starkman, Allyse Gastep, Michelle Vinokurov, Garrett Winters, Daria Yudina, and Denis Yudin. Their insights are reflected throughout this text, helping to ensure that our recommendations offer an inclusive and compassionate approach. Finally, and with a lot of love, we'd like to thank our immensely supportive friends and family who have supported and encouraged us throughout this project.

First published 2024

Behavior Essentials, Visualized is a product of ABA Visualized.

Written by:
Morgan van Diepen, M.Ed., BCBA & Janna Bedoyan, M.Ed., NBCT

Design and Art Direction by:
Boudewijn van Diepen

Illustrations by:
Saliha Caliskan

Edited by:
Rose M. Reynolds

www.ABAVisualized.com
info@ABAVisualized.com

ISBN: 979-8-218-41538-9

Contents

Note From the Authors

We believe in the power of great teaching. We recognize the challenges you face every day, and we understand the need for practical, effective strategies for managing classrooms and influencing student behavior.

We've visualized each evidence-based behavior strategy as relatable and actionable because we hope to see them ripple through classrooms, fostering environments where every student has the chance to flourish.

Our goal is that this book extends beyond being merely a guide—it aims to become your trusted ally. We want the strategies within to not only leap off the pages but also seamlessly integrate into your classrooms, turning challenges into victories and concerns into confidence. As teachers navigate the complexities of supporting many students with many different needs, this book is designed to provide you with guidance in creating inclusive environments where every student can thrive.

Thank you for all that you do,

Janna Bedoyan

About the Authors

Morgan van Diepen

Morgan is a Board Certified Behavior Analyst (BCBA) and Autism Specialist with over 15 years of working experience in the fields of Applied Behavior Analysis (ABA) and Special Education. Through her international experience working with families and schools, Morgan saw the need for more approachable behavior expertise, and this became her passion. As a self-published author and behavior expert, she has presented at several national conferences and continues to act as an advocate for accessible expertise for educators and families.

Janna Bedoyan

Janna is an Autism Early Childhood Education Teacher with 15 years of experience in the classroom. She is a National Board Certified Teacher (NBCT) and Augmentative and Alternative Communication (AAC) Specialist. She is deeply passionate about AAC, as she has spent much of her career helping children and their families find ways to communicate together. Her dedication, expertise, and genuine love for what she does make her an invaluable educator and advocate for autistic students. She understands that each child is unique and requires individualized support to reach their full potential. She is an outstanding educator who exudes empathy and compassion in everything she does. Her love for her students shines through in every interaction, making her a beloved teacher among students and their families.

Bou van Diepen

Boudewijn (Bou) is an award-winning designer who approaches every project from a conceptual and original perspective. His ability to effectively shape complex information into an understandable and aesthetically attractive visual is evidenced through his more than 10 years of diverse experience ranging from projects for government agencies to start-up nonprofit organizations. Bou loves to use his creativity to make the world a more approachable place.

Our Mission

Our mission with *Behavior Essentials, Visualized: A Teacher's Visual Guide to Supporting Students with Diverse Needs* is to provide effective strategies that are approachable, accessible, and relatable so that teachers feel prepared and confident in fully supporting their students. We understand that managing classrooms and student behavior can be overwhelming and challenging at times. That's why we have created this book, to simplify the process and offer practical solutions for teachers. Our goal is to help you create a classroom where students feel safe, engaged, and motivated to learn.

We aim to provide comprehensive support, visual strategies, and resources tailored to teachers, enabling them to enhance their teaching practices, feel prepared to handle challenges that arise in their classrooms, and feel confident in selecting and implementing behavior strategies. We hope this guidebook helps create positive learning environments for all students.

Empower

We aim to empower teachers to implement impactful and inclusive teaching strategies, nurturing a supportive learning atmosphere for all students. As the guiding force in your classroom, we aim to equip you with the confidence to autonomously make decisions that align with the needs of both you and your students. We trust in your expertise and familiarity with your students' unique qualities. This classroom is yours, and your insight into your students is unparalleled.

Enhance

We strive to enhance teachers' confidence in managing diverse classroom settings, building student engagement, and success. With our visual strategies, we hope you learn new ideas to fostering student motivation, proactively prevent challenging behaviors, and teach essential skills that help students thrive.

Encourage

We hope to encourage a community of support and sharing of best practices among teachers, service providers, paraprofessionals, and support staff leading to continuous improvement in the quality of education and support for students with diverse needs.

Book Overview

In the following chapters, you will learn how to use evidence-based behavior strategies to improve your students' skill development as well as prevent and reduce challenging behaviors. The step-by-step visual strategies are organized by the following chapters:

- Building Motivation: Proactive approaches to enhancing student engagement
- Preventing Challenging Behaviors: Classwide and individual strategies that aim to set students up for success
- Teaching New Skills: Versatile strategies for building essential skills
- Responding to Challenging Behaviors: Strategies for supporting students using a calm and compassionate approach
- Template & Tools: A custom-made collection of blank visual templates and tools to use alongside the strategies!

Who Can Use

Behavior Essentials, Visualized was created for all teachers. Our aim is to equip you with tools that empower you to effectively support students with diverse behavioral and learning needs. Through the following visual strategies, we provide solutions for common classroom concerns. These strategies were chosen for their proven effectiveness in school settings and their adaptability. Each strategy features characters referred to as "teacher" and "student" to encompass various individuals involved in teaching and learning, such as teachers, paraprofessionals, and service providers, across students of different age groups. We encourage all those supporting the student to utilize these strategies. *Behavior Essentials, Visualized* is designed for use in educational settings spanning from preschool to adult transition programs. Whether in special education, inclusion, or general education classrooms, our resources aim to create environments where all students can succeed.

How to Use

This book serves as more than just a guide—it becomes your ally. Use it in the way that helps you and your team the most! You can read it from start to finish and revisit strategies that resonate most with you. Alternatively, you may refer to the chart of strategies in the subsequent pages to pinpoint a strategy that can address your current focus or priority. We would recommend starting with reading the Foundations chapter to establish the essentials that will enhance the effectiveness of the strategies.

Each visual strategy featured in this book is an evidence-based strategy, meaning they have met rigorous criteria showing that they are useful, of high quality, and effective for many different individuals. We have illustrated a common scenario of what each strategy looks like in a real-life situation. While these strategies are versatile and applicable across various school settings and scenarios, you can refer to the "Context" text on each to have guidance on their best use and the "Tip" section to read about potential variations. In the visual strategies, you'll see colored arrows connecting the steps. A white arrow guides the teacher preparation steps, green arrows indicate the student's engagement in the positive behavior, and red arrows highlight the pathway when a student engages in challenging behavior.

As you become more comfortable integrating the strategies into your classroom routines, you can start "stacking" them, using multiple strategies at a time, often resulting in even greater student success. We encourage you to share these visual strategies with your team to promote consistent support for the student. To make this book a comprehensive tool, we've also included a collection of templates and tools that align with the strategies. Feel free to make copies of these resources and use them in your classroom!

What to Expect?

The strategies featured in the following chapters have all been shown to be effective; however, you may see success at different rates. Also, each strategy may not be appropriate for each student. Consider your student's strengths, preferences, emotional and sensory needs, and how they learn best! The best way to utilize the strategies to create impactful behavior change and see results is to be consistent. Once you've identified a strategy that works well for your student, expand on how you could use that strategy to build other skills or help in other challenging situations. For example, if you are using the Providing Choices strategy to help your student feel encouraged to join a whole group lesson, try using this strategy to help with initiating independent tasks next! Additionally, collaborate with other service providers, paraprofessionals, general education teachers, and other Individualized Education Program (IEP) team members to share ideas on using this strategy in new ways to best support your student. Be consistent and patient; changing behavior takes time!

Strategies based on function of behavior	Access	Attention	Escape	Sensory
BUILDING MOTIVATION				
Building Rapport, page 106	✓	✓	✓	✓
First, Then, page 108	✓		✓	
Providing Choices, page 110			✓	✓
Whole Class Reward System, page 112	✓		✓	
3 Reward Options, page 114	✓	✓	✓	✓
Token Boards, page 116	✓		✓	
Range of Rewards, page 118	✓	✓	✓	✓
Check-In, Check-Out, page 120	✓	✓	✓	
Individual Points Plan, page 122	✓		✓	
PREVENTING CHALLENGING BEHAVIORS				
Classroom Setup, page 128	✓	✓	✓	✓
Priming, page 130	✓		✓	✓
Power Card, page 132	✓	✓	✓	✓
Easy, Easy, Hard, page 134			✓	
A Better Way to Say "No", page 136	✓			
Visual Schedule, page 138	✓		✓	✓
Break Tickets, page 140			✓	
Scheduled Breaks/Connections, page 142			✓	
TEACHING NEW SKILLS				
Modeling, page 154	✓	✓	✓	✓
Shaping, page 156	✓	✓	✓	✓
Fading, page 158				
Breaking Down Skills, page 160				
Choice Mapping, page 162	✓	✓	✓	✓
Building Better Behaviors, page 164	✓	✓	✓	✓
Teaching to Request, page 166	✓	✓	✓	✓
Problem Solving, page 168	✓	✓	✓	✓
Self-Advocacy, page 170	✓	✓	✓	✓
Self-Regulation, page 172	✓	✓	✓	✓
Introducing Communication, page 174				
RESPONDING TO CHALLENGING BEHAVIORS				
Tell, Show, Help, page 184	✓	✓	✓	
Firm, but Flexible, page 186	✓	✓	✓	
Pause, Redirect, Reward, page 188	✓	✓	✓	✓
Blocking Unsafe Behaviors, page 190	✓	✓	✓	✓
Managing Self-Injurious Behaviors, page 192	✓	✓	✓	✓
Escalation Plan, page 194	✓	✓	✓	✓
Rebuilding Rapport, page 196	✓	✓	✓	✓

Strategies based on priority

	Build a positive & inclusive classroom culture	Build motivation for individual students	Reduce classwide challenging behaviors	Reduce challenging behaviors for individual students	Build student independence & self-advocacy
BUILDING MOTIVATION					
Building Rapport, page 106	✓	✓	✓	✓	✓
First, Then, page 108	✓	✓	✓	✓	
Providing Choices, page 110	✓	✓	✓	✓	✓
Whole Class Reward System, page 112	✓		✓		
3 Reward Options, page 114		✓		✓	✓
Token Boards, page 116		✓		✓	✓
Range of Rewards, page 118	✓	✓	✓	✓	✓
Check-In, Check-Out, page 120		✓		✓	
Individual Points Plan, page 122		✓		✓	✓
PREVENTING CHALLENGING BEHAVIORS					
Classroom Setup, page 128	✓	✓	✓	✓	✓
Priming, page 130	✓		✓	✓	
Power Card, page 132	✓	✓		✓	✓
Easy, Easy, Hard, page 134	✓		✓	✓	
A Better Way to Say "No", page 136				✓	
Visual Schedule, page 138	✓	✓	✓	✓	✓
Break Tickets, page 140				✓	✓
Scheduled Breaks/Connections, page 142	✓		✓	✓	
TEACHING NEW SKILLS					
Modeling, page 154	✓		✓	✓	✓
Shaping, page 156	✓	✓		✓	✓
Fading, page 158					✓
Breaking Down Skills, page 160	✓		✓		✓
Choice Mapping, page 162		✓		✓	✓
Building Better Behaviors, page 164	✓		✓	✓	✓
Teaching to Request, page 166				✓	✓
Problem Solving, page 168			✓	✓	✓
Self-Advocacy, page 170	✓			✓	✓
Self-Regulation, page 172	✓		✓	✓	✓
Introducing Communication, page 174	✓			✓	✓
RESPONDING TO CHALLENGING BEHAVIORS					
Tell, Show, Help, page 184				✓	✓
Firm, but Flexible, page 186	✓	✓	✓	✓	
Pause, Redirect, Reward, page 188				✓	
Blocking Unsafe Behaviors, page 190				✓	✓
Managing Self-Injurious Behaviors, page 192				✓	
Escalation Plan, page 194				✓	✓
Rebuilding Rapport, page 196	✓		✓	✓	

Foundations

Introduction

In this chapter, we provide guidance on creating a classroom environment where students feel engaged and ready to learn. Before diving into behavior strategies, it is important to understand the impact of such an environment. We discuss the importance of embracing trauma-informed approaches and understanding the reasons behind challenging behaviors.

To prepare you for incorporating behavior strategies into your classroom practice, we have included approachable guides to behavior plans, making recommendations, and IEP collaboration, as well as supporting paraprofessionals. Our aim is to help you lay the foundation for a positive classroom culture where all students can excel, empowering you to effectively teach.

Behavioral Approach to Supporting Students

We understand that every day in the classroom presents unique challenges and triumphs. It's common to feel isolated in these experiences, yet within this guidebook lie strategies and scenarios illustrated to empower and equip you. These tools will help you transition from merely surviving to truly thriving, fostering confidence in your role as the classroom leader and in the day-to-day decisions you make.

In recognizing the profound influence teachers have on student success, it's crucial to understand the role of behavioral support in fostering a learning environment where each student feels valued and seen. Even in the face of challenging behaviors such as disrespect or aggression, it's the teacher's support that can transform these moments into opportunities for student growth and self-confidence.

It's important to recognize that when we help students improve their behaviors, that impact directly connects to their academic success, social relationships, and self-esteem. One of the key reasons for taking a behavioral approach to supporting students is that behavioral success often leads to academic success. When a student is able to self-regulate, self-advocate, and communicate effectively, they are better able to focus on learning and engaging with the curriculum.

Understanding the individual needs of each student includes taking into account their academic strengths, preferences and interests, emotional well-being, and any potential challenges they may face in the learning environment. By having this knowledge, teachers can tailor interventions and support plans to meet the needs of each student.

Furthermore, improving behaviors can also have a positive impact on a student's peer interactions and social skills. Students who exhibit challenging behaviors may struggle to form positive relationships with their peers, leading to feelings of isolation and loneliness. By helping students develop essential social skills like communication, collaboration, and problem solving, we can help our students build meaningful relationships.

Taking a behavioral approach also has positive effects on a student's self-esteem. When students are able to control their behavior and make positive choices, they experience feelings of accomplishment and increased self-worth. This can have a significant impact on their overall well-being and improve their overall attitude toward school.

Collaboration among teachers, families, service providers, and other professionals is essential in implementing an effective behavioral support plan for our students. By working together as a team, stakeholders can share insights about the student's needs, coordinate interventions across different settings, and provide consistent support. This collaborative approach ensures that each individual involved in the student's education is aligned in their efforts to promote positive behaviors and maximize the student's learning.

In this book, we will show ways to improve behaviors and teach essential skills that can help boost students' academic success, improve peer relationships, and build confidence in school settings. We want to emphasize the importance of collaboration among service providers to maximize the impact on students with diverse needs. When all of this is in place, our students, no matter their age, can grow into resilient, independent individuals who have the necessary tools to succeed in school and beyond. A quote shared by Alex Baughns, an autistic self-advocate and collaborator on this book, highlights this importance:

"An autistic child becomes an autistic adult. When they're in school, they should be provided resources and support to help the autistic child thrive as an adult."

House
By: Alex Baughns

Your parents give you the building blocks
Your teachers give you the cement to build it up
The people you surround it with are your neighbors
When this is set up, you can decorate your house and live beautifully

We love this poem from Alex. It beautifully illustrates that when autistic individuals have strong foundations, they can then design their lives in ways that are fulfilling and authentic to them, which is what we all deserve.

Research: It's Not Your Fault!

Recent research revealed that only about one-third of educators receive adequate training to address challenging behaviors, leading to over 40% of teachers feeling ill-prepared to manage classroom dynamics and student behavior. This gap doesn't stem from teachers' lack of dedication but rather from significant shortcomings in comprehensive classroom and behavior management training within teaching programs. It's concerning that merely 15% of special education programs provide thorough classroom management training.

The emotional demands of supporting a variety of students with a variety of needs with limited training to do so often leads to exhaustion and frustration for teachers. This burnout frequently drives teachers out of the field, resulting in a shortage of qualified educators and depriving student teachers of experienced mentors. Research shows that the extent of burnout experienced by teachers is closely tied to their proficiency and comfortability with classroom management. When a classroom feels chaotic and the teacher finds it challenging to sustain an engaged learning environment, teachers often feel the impacts. These may include emotional exhaustion, struggles with regulating emotions, feelings of disconnect, negative attitudes toward students, and a significant decrease in job satisfaction.

In one study, 55% of teachers reported that they were thinking about leaving the field of teaching.

Inadequate classroom and behavior management training not only impacts teachers but also significantly affects students, especially those with diverse needs. Without the essential skills for effective classroom management, teachers may struggle to create an inclusive and supportive learning environment. This lack of training can lead to burnout, particularly among special education teachers. Studies show that special education teachers are 11% more likely to leave their positions and 72% more likely to switch schools compared to general education teachers. Recent data from the School Pulse Survey reveals that 44% of elementary, middle, high, and combined-grade schools nationwide report double the vacancy rates in special education compared to other positions. This is why we developed *Behavior Essentials, Visualized*. Our aim is to offer resources and practical tools, along with real-life examples, to support effective classroom management and reduce burnout, ultimately retaining experienced and impactful teachers.

Classroom Management vs. Behavior Management

Classroom management and behavior management are interconnected, and both are crucial in shaping a positive learning environment. Classroom management establishes clear boundaries and expectations, while behavior management provides individualized support for each student's development. Tailoring strategies to address the specific needs in your classroom ensures students can thrive academically and behaviorally. Classwide behavior management strategies involve implementing consistent strategies across the entire class to foster a positive and inclusive learning environment. By setting clear expectations, setting motivating rewards, and prioritizing proactive approaches, teachers promote student engagement and can prevent many unwanted behaviors. Behavior management focuses on understanding each student individually, recognizing their unique needs and potential triggers. This individual support approach often involves developing plans such as Behavior Intervention Plans (BIPs) to address challenging behaviors.

Classroom Management

- Includes classwide behavior strategies
- Promotes active engagement
- Considers seating arrangements
- Focuses on the overall environment
- Differentiated instructional strategies
- Involves establishing expectations
- Emphasizes creating a conducive learning space
- Sets the tone and culture of a classroom
- Promotes participation & academic achievement
- Organization of the classroom
- Routines clearly established

Behavior Management

- Individualized strategies based on student-specific needs
- Focuses on reinforcing positive behavior
- Targets specific student behaviors
- May include a Behavior Intervention Plan
- May include behavior service minutes to support instruction and behavior management
- Addresses disruptive or challenging behaviors
- Prioritizes preventative and skill-building strategies
- May include a goal to reduce certain behaviors
- May include a skill-building goal

Understanding a Tiered Approach to Student Support

Support tiers within a school-wide system are designed to meet the varying needs of students to ensure everyone's educational success. Recognizing that each student's needs are unique, a tiered support system provides a structured approach to delivering the right level of help. All students start in Tier 1 support services. Based on individual needs and progress, some students may qualify for Tier 2 interventions, while others may require Tier 3 specialized support. The tiered system allows for a cumulative approach to addressing varying levels of student needs.

Tiered Approach to Student Support

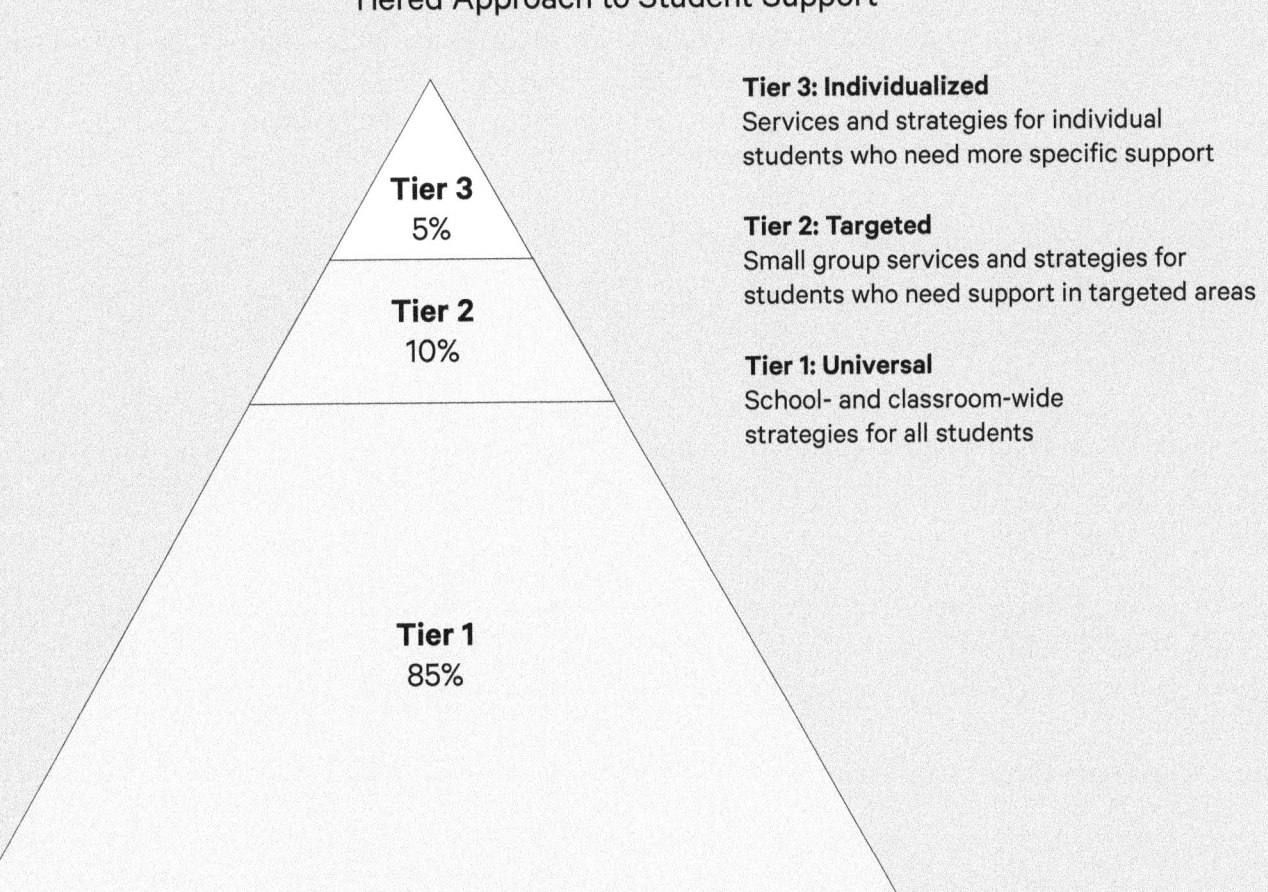

Tier 3: Individualized
Services and strategies for individual students who need more specific support

Tier 2: Targeted
Small group services and strategies for students who need support in targeted areas

Tier 1: Universal
School- and classroom-wide strategies for all students

Tier 3
5%

Tier 2
10%

Tier 1
85%

Tier 1: Universal Support

Tier 1 represents foundational support that benefits all students. This includes school- and classroom-wide strategies that all students receive. In practical terms, 85% of students thrive with these broad support strategies. These universal supports are designed to create a positive and inclusive school climate that promotes academic achievement and overall well-being for all students.

This includes

- Schoolwide Positive Behavior Supports (PBIS): A school-wide approach that focuses on creating a positive environment and teaching students appropriate behaviors through proactive supports and rewards. Examples include visual supports placed around the school, school-wide reward systems, and points or "money" redeemable at school stores.
- Core Academic Instruction: Where all students receive the same curriculum with high-quality teaching methods and teacher professional development is prioritized.
- Clear Expectations: Schools establish consistent rules and routines that are practiced consistently in all areas of the school.
- Classwide Strategies: Teachers use evidence-based instructional and behavior management strategies for the entire class. Examples include clearly posted schedules, visual supports, transition reminders, whole-class rewards, scheduled breaks, and designated calm corners.
- Clubs and Organizations: A school-wide initiative to cater to different interests and talents of students by offering community service opportunities, cultural celebrations, and clubs relating to students' strengths and interests.

Tier 2: Targeted Support

Tier 2 interventions offer additional support to students who may need more targeted assistance with academics, behavior, and/or social-emotional skills. These interventions are typically provided in small groups, but could also include schoolwide programs that aim to reach students who require more support. About 10% of students would benefit from Tier 2 supports in addition to the Tier 1 strategies already in place.

This includes

- Targeted Academic Services: Pull-out services for specialized instruction in reading, writing, and math.
- Social and Emotional Skill-Building Groups or Services: Small group sessions focused on developing specific social skills such as conflict resolution, self-regulation, and conversation skills.

- Check-In, Check-Out (CICO): At a Tier 2 level of support, this strategy would be set up schoolwide where the administration establishes three to five behavioral expectations for all students. All students are paired with a staff member to meet briefly with at the beginning and end of each school day. In the morning meeting, the staff member reminds them of their expectations and provides encouragement. In the afternoon meeting, the students self-reflect to share if they felt they met those expectations that day or need to discuss areas they feel they can improve on.
- Active Supervision and Pre-Corrections: School staff are strategically placed around the school to provide positive and proactive reminders of school expectations.
- Restorative Justice Circles: Structured small group meetings that aim to foster a supportive school community and manage conflict and tensions by discussing harm and restoring relationships.

Tier 3: Individualized Support

Tier 3 provides a customized structure for students who require more support than what they are receiving with Tier 1 and Tier 2. This includes individualized instruction and interventions tailored to the student's specific needs. About 5% of students need individualized strategies, including Tier 3 support like counseling, behavior services, and specialized instruction, aimed at improving behavior, academic success, and overall well-being.

This includes
- Functional Behavior Assessment (FBA): A process used to identify the underlying factors contributing to a student's behavior and develop a behavior intervention plan.
- Behavior Intervention Plan (BIP): A written plan that outlines evidence-based behavior strategies specifically chosen to meet an individual student's needs. Students who engage in challenging behaviors that impede their learning or have the potential to cause harm would benefit from having a curated BIP developed for them. (See "An Approachable Guide to FBAs," pg. 75 to learn more.)
- Individualized Education Program (IEP): For students with disabilities, an IEP can address both academic and behavioral goals and provide accommodations and modifications as needed.
- Counseling/Therapy: Mental health services that offer tailored support in developing social-emotional skills.
- Wraparound Services: Coordinated support and services from various professionals, agencies, and community resources to address all aspects of a student's life.

Understanding & Celebrating Neurodiversity

Introduction to Neurodiversity

Neurodiversity is a concept that embraces differences in the human brain as being natural, normal, and not "less than" those without these differences. When talking about individuals with disabilities, we want to be sure to use accepting and normalizing terms. If an individual has a developmental disability (like Autism, ADHD, or Dyslexia), their thought patterns, behaviors, or learning styles may fall outside of what is considered "normal" or "neurotypical." We can instead say that they are "neurodiverse" or "neurodivergent." This framework celebrates individuality, and many self-advocates express pride in their neurodiverse ways of thinking and behaving!

While there is no official statistic of how many people are neurodiverse, ADHD Aware estimates the number of people with neurodivergent disorders as over 30% of the population. If you'd like to learn how to become a more-informed advocate for the neurodiversity movement and community, we recommend the book *Demystifying Disability* by Emily Ladau.

Since the term neurodiversity was first introduced in 1997 by autistic sociologist Judy Singer, the autistic community has widely embraced its framework as it recognizes the strengths that also come with having a diagnosis. Whether you are neurotypical or neurodiverse yourself, we encourage you to share this perspective as well.

For an individual to receive a diagnosis, there must be a set of concerns that result in significant difficulty, distress, and/or impairment in a person's life compared to the neurotypical population. We also know that these diagnoses have many strengths attributed to them! If you are or know someone who is neurodiverse, you surely can recognize these beautiful aspects! In the following texts, we have selected four of the diagnoses that are commonly seen in students with diverse needs to explain a bit further.

Autism

Autism Spectrum Disorder (ASD) refers to a developmental diagnosis including notable impacts on social skills, speech, and communication and engagement in repetitive behaviors or focal interests. Individuals may present a wide range of abilities and challenges, leading to the understanding of Autism occurring on a spectrum. During play, children with ASD may often focus on their restricted interests or repetitive behavior. Having restricted interests can actually lead to finding meaningful hobbies and careers. However, they may also create limited opportunities for peer interaction and friendships to develop if there are not many peers who share those same interests. In regards to social and play skills, a way to support those with ASD is to teach skills that enhance peer relationships while also celebrating their unique interests.

A common presentation of Autism in young learners is a language delay. In fact, recent research has suggested that about 25% of individuals with Autism are nonvocal or "minimally verbal," which was defined as using fewer than 30 functional vocal words or being unable to use speech alone to communicate. It's important to remember that although someone is not communicating vocally, this does not mean that they cannot understand or cannot learn. With the growing access to Autism support services for clients and families, there is more awareness of the benefits of introducing Augmentative and Alternative Communication (AAC) as a powerful tool for giving these students' a voice. AAC includes all forms of communication other than vocal speech, including but not limited to sign language, the use of speech-generating devices (AAC devices), and visuals. Introducing AAC can help bridge the gap between our learners' inner thoughts and the outside world and help them develop stronger bonds with others, allowing them to feel more included in the world around them. AAC has truly changed the lives of many autistic people for the better! If you would like to learn more about AAC and strategies for building communication, we recommend checking out our book, *AAC Visualized*, which was created in collaboration with AAC specialists, SLPs, autistic self-advocates AAC users, and other experts in this field.

Early Signs of Autism

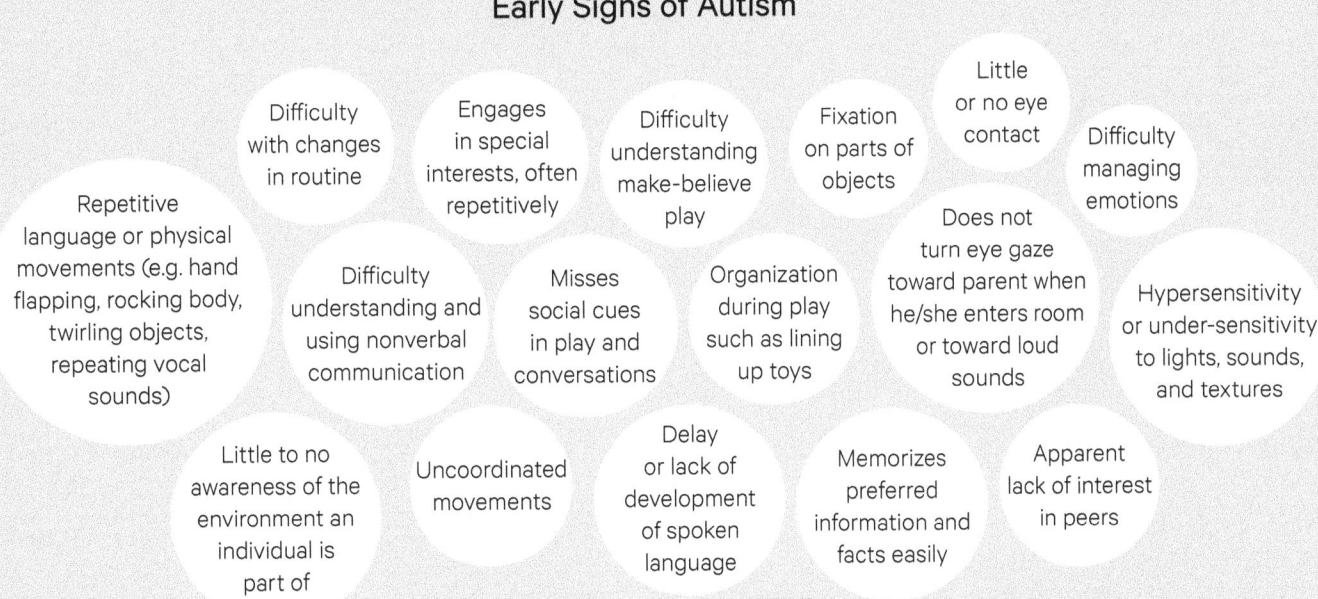

Difficulty with changes in routine

Engages in special interests, often repetitively

Difficulty understanding make-believe play

Fixation on parts of objects

Little or no eye contact

Difficulty managing emotions

Repetitive language or physical movements (e.g. hand flapping, rocking body, twirling objects, repeating vocal sounds)

Difficulty understanding and using nonverbal communication

Misses social cues in play and conversations

Organization during play such as lining up toys

Does not turn eye gaze toward parent when he/she enters room or toward loud sounds

Hypersensitivity or under-sensitivity to lights, sounds, and textures

Little to no awareness of the environment an individual is part of

Uncoordinated movements

Delay or lack of development of spoken language

Memorizes preferred information and facts easily

Apparent lack of interest in peers

Recent increased Autism awareness has led to increased prevalence rates (currently 1 in 36). In addition, early diagnosis has led to early access to individualized services and supports, which have significantly improved individuals' and their families' lives. Autism awareness has grown so much lately that autistic self-advocates have proposed changing April's "Autism Awareness" month to "Autism Acceptance" month, suggesting that our focus should shift to accepting and celebrating these neurodiversities!

Causes of Autism

While there is not a proven cause of ASD, recent research indicates genetics is a significant contributing factor. A report by the Autism Society of America concluded that Autism has no racial, ethnic, or social boundaries and that family income, lifestyle, and education level do not affect the chance of Autism occurrence. In 2014, a comprehensive and influential research study evaluating the familial risk of Autism was published by Sven Sandin and his research team. Their results showed strong evidence for heritability and genetic influence in individuals with Autism. They determined the risk of an individual having Autism was ten times greater when the individual had a sibling with Autism versus an individual with no sibling diagnosis. An individual with a cousin diagnosed with Autism would be two times more likely also to receive the diagnosis. Overall, Sandin and his team estimated Autism hereditability to be 50%. In summary, the most accepted belief relating to the impact of genetics is that genes play an influential role in the diagnosis of Autism; however, it may not be an absolute role. Ongoing genetic research hopes to identify a clear biological cause which may help with reducing stigma and finding new ways to better support this population.

Let's talk about the "Spectrum" in "Autism Spectrum Disorder." Picture it as a line stretching from one impact level to another, marked by designations such as "low-functioning" at one end and "high-functioning" at the other. It initially seems straightforward, doesn't it? But how can a single line possibly encompass the full complexity of autistic experiences?

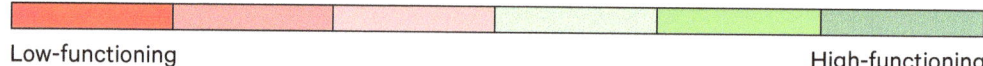

Low-functioning   High-functioning

The limitations within this spectrum are significant. Terms like "low-functioning" or "high-functioning" can inaccurately depict an individual's reality. These labels bring with them preconceived notions and oversimplifications, often causing more harm than good to those they seek to define. Further, labels not only fail to encompass the intricate spectrum of autistic experiences but also perpetuate damaging stereotypes, obstacles, and barriers. By fixating on perceived levels of functionality, there's a risk of disregarding the individual's unique strengths, struggles, and needs. Instead, we must adopt a language of understanding and respect. Terms like "support needs" offer a more accurate and compassionate perspective. They encourage us to consider the specific assistance an individual requires in certain areas while acknowledging their capabilities and potential in others. This shift in terminology from "functioning" to "support needs" aligns with our commitment to listen to self-advocates and adjust our practices and language accordingly.

Instead of thinking of the Autism spectrum as linear from "less autistic" to "more autistic," we encourage you to view it more like a spectrum color wheel. By inviting the autistic student to color in their areas of strength and need for more support, we are providing a tool for them to articulate their experiences, which can help guide us in knowing where to support. It's not about measuring up to external expectations; it's about expressing oneself authentically. This approach acknowledges that each autistic person's profile is as unique as anyone else. In our Tools chapter, you'll find blank color wheels that you can invite your autistic students to complete.

An Autism Spectrum Color Wheel

This is a sample of how an autistic person could fill in their own color wheel, reflecting on areas of their life that they feel are impacted the most.

1. No impact on my quality of life
2. Occasional but minimal impact
3. Sometimes, but easy to manage
4. Regularly interferes
5. Significantly affects my daily functioning and overall well-being

"We all come in all shapes and hues. This is art."

Alex Baughns, autistic self-advocate

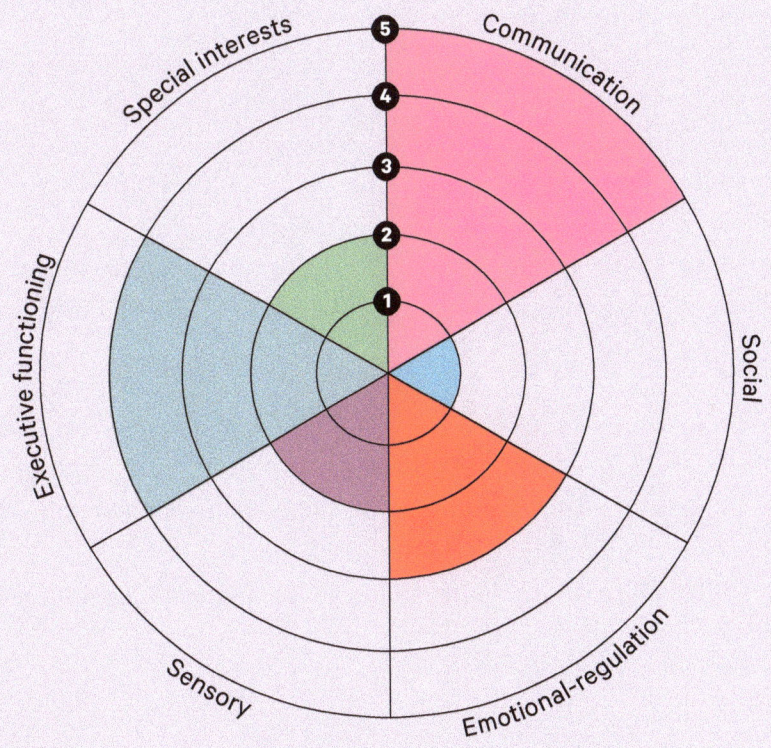

Down Syndrome

Down Syndrome (DS), also known as Trisomy 21, is a condition in which a person is born with an extra chromosome (chromosome 21). Currently, Down Syndrome cannot be prevented, but it can be detected during pregnancy. Although individuals with Down Syndrome may look similar, each person has unique characteristics and personalities. Individuals often experience developmental delays; thus, it is important to foster the development of strengths and talents in congruence with basic skills. Children with Down Syndrome may need assistance with self-care, including bathing, dressing, and grooming. The Center for Disease Control and Prevention states the current rate of Down Syndrome as 1 in 700 births in the United States, making Down Syndrome the most common chromosomal condition. Behavioral and occupational therapy services have shown to be effective at helping individuals with Down Syndrome develop a range of skills, including self-advocacy skills, safety skills, and self-care skills (such as brushing teeth and getting dressed), as well as building executive functioning skills (such as problem solving and planning).

Early Signs of Down Syndrome

Low muscle tone (hypotonia) and slower growth rate compared to typical peers

Flat facial profile with upward slant to the eyes, smaller than average size ears, and a protruding tongue

Increased risk for comorbid diseases (including congenital heart defect, pulmonary hypertension, and hearing and vision challenges)

Mild to moderate intellectual impairment

ADHD

Attention Deficit Hyperactivity Disorder (ADHD) is one of the most common neurodevelopmental diagnoses in childhood, occurring in 10% of children aged 3-17 in the United States. Typically, children are diagnosed in their early school years due to trouble paying attention, controlling impulsive behaviors, or being overly active. For individuals with ADHD, these problems are persistent and interfere with academic and social life. The key behaviors of ADHD are inattention and hyperactivity/impulsivity. People with ADHD might only face one of these behavioral concerns, while others may have combined challenges. While the specific cause of ADHD is unknown, current research shows that genetics plays an important role in its prevalence. Alternatively, research does not support the views that ADHD can be caused by a high-sugar diet, watching too much television, parenting styles, or environmental factors including family dynamics and poverty. The symptoms of ADHD can change over time as a person ages; thus, it is essential to teach specific skills that can reduce the challenges these individuals may face. For example, individuals could be taught specific strategies for organization and time management or self-advocating for breaks and accommodations as needed.

Common Signs of ADHD

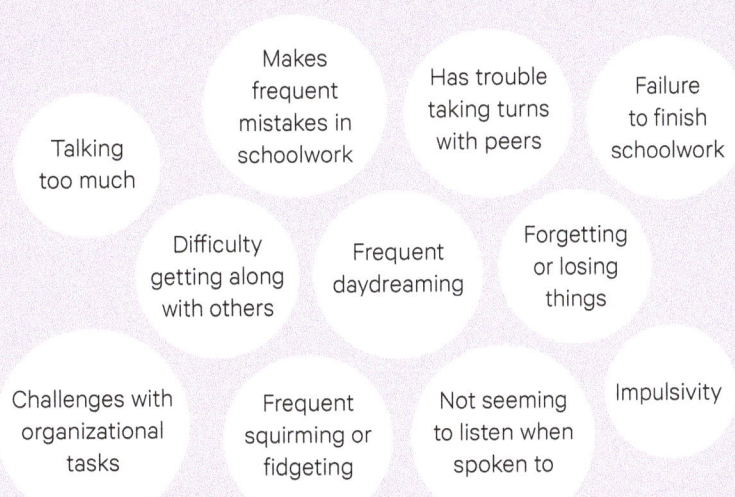

OCD

Obsessive-Compulsive Disorder (OCD) is an anxiety-related disorder in which individuals have recurring, unwanted thoughts, ideas, or sensations (obsessions), that make them feel driven to do something repetitively (compulsions). In individuals with OCD, compelling behaviors take up a significant amount of time (more than one hour each day) and commonly interfere with other daily activities. Children often report that they do these behaviors in order to prevent something bad from happening or to "make them feel better."

OCD equally affects men, women, and children of all races and socioeconomic backgrounds at a rate of about 1 in 100 children. Individuals with OCD may also experience anxiety, depression, or increased engagement in disruptive behaviors. The cause of OCD is unknown; however, current research is supporting genetic and hereditary factors. Within behavior services, a branch called Acceptance and Commitment Therapy (ACT) has been showing promising outcomes in supporting individuals with mental health disorders such as anxiety, PTSD, and OCD to better manage their symptoms.

Common Themes of Obsessions

- Need for things to be in an orderly and symmetrical manner
- Extreme thoughts of harming self or others
- Unwanted and pervasive thoughts, including aggression or sexual urges
- Fear of contamination

Common Themes of Compulsion

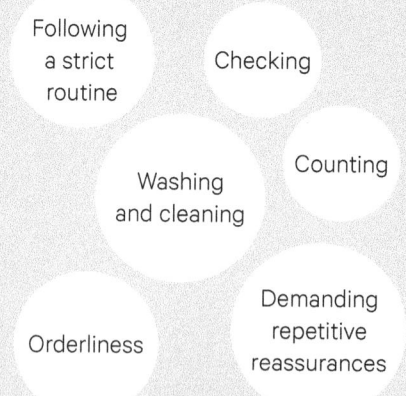

- Following a strict routine
- Checking
- Counting
- Washing and cleaning
- Orderliness
- Demanding repetitive reassurances

Understanding and Celebrating Neurodiversity as a Teacher

In the landscape of education, understanding and celebrating neurodiversity is paramount for creating inclusive classrooms where every student can flourish. Neurodiversity celebrates the uniqueness of every individual's brain, challenging the notion of a "normal" brain. It advocates for the acceptance and inclusion of individuals with brain-based disabilities, including Autism, learning disabilities, and mental health conditions. The neurodiversity movement champions their rightful place in society alongside neurotypical individuals.

As teachers, our primary mission is to establish an environment that is both safe and welcoming for every student. A key strategy in achieving this is to embrace neurodivergence, which involves recognizing and honoring the unique strengths and talents of neurodivergent students. These individuals often have different methods of processing information and communicating, but "different" does not mean "inferior." By understanding these differences and adapting your teaching strategies accordingly, you can create a more inclusive learning environment where all students feel heard and respected. It's essential for both teachers and administrators to promote a neurodiverse-accepting school climate, where differences are celebrated.

Celebrating neurodiversity involves recognizing and appreciating the inherent value and potential of every student. Embracing neurodiversity requires valuing diversity, promoting empathy, and celebrating human experience. By integrating these principles into our teaching philosophy, we create inclusive environments that empower all students to excel. Promoting empathy and understanding among students reinforces acceptance and cultivates compassion. Research shows that fostering a neurodiverse-affirming environment enhances students' self-esteem, confidence, and academic achievement. Embracing neurodiversity not only promotes diversity and inclusion but also fosters a culture of respect and celebration of individual differences. We encourage you to integrate the following seven practices into your teaching philosophy. These practices were crafted in close collaboration with numerous neurodiverse self-advocates (see "Acknowledgements"). We feel honored to compile their recommendations and share their insights with you.

7 Neurodiversity-Affirming Practices for Teachers

1. Utilize a Strength-Based Approach

The strength-based approach to teaching emphasizes abilities, knowledge, and capacities over areas of need. It's a powerful strategy where educators prioritize understanding a student's strengths, knowledge, and passions and seamlessly integrate them into their teaching. Extending this into students' Individualized Education Programs (IEPs) is imperative. For example, the Present Levels section of the IEP is the perfect place to highlight a student's joys, special interests, and strengths. Then, the team can lead collaborative discussions about how to incorporate these strengths into learning to promote individualized academic success. When writing IEP goals, the focus should be on meeting the student's needs, not forcing them to act or be neurotypical. It's time to end goals that require eye contact or reducing nonharmful sefl-stimulatory behaviors.

> "Stimming is how I express myself."
>
> Alex Baughns

Instead of viewing neurodiverse students through a "deficit" lens, it is crucial to highlight their strengths and abilities. By focusing on what they can do rather than what they struggle with, we can empower them to be embraced for their individuality and thrive. For example, instead of saying, "He is nonverbal," we can say, "He communicates through alternative methods such as sign language or AAC devices." This shift in language not only changes perceptions but also promotes a positive outlook on the capabilities of our students and normalized differences.

> "Remind individuals what makes them special, unique, and capable of succeeding rather than focusing on challenges or barriers. Continue to highlight their successes, especially when someone is feeling the weight of the challenges that may be around them."
>
> Denis Yudin

The below table outlines words and phrases that are still commonly heard when talking about students with diverse needs. These terms can have damaging impacts on how others view neurodiverse students and how they view themselves. Alex Baughns, an autistic self-advocate who collaborated with us on this book, shares her recommendations for strength-based language we should use instead.

Instead of saying this	Use this strength-based language
Rigid	Passionate, dedicated, and persistent
Restricted interest	Knowledgable and curious about
Off in their own world or spacecadet	Imaginative and creative
Weird or nerdy	Fascinating, eccentric, and individualistic
Stimming or hyperactive	Animated

Teaching students that not all differences or disabilities are visible promotes inclusivity and acceptance of everyone. Encouraging students to explore topics they're passionate about, such as Temple Grandin's revolutionary work in animal agriculture or Barbara McClintock's groundbreaking genetic research on corn, showcases the value of diverse interests and abilities. Similarly, highlighting Satoshi Tajiri's journey from hyperfocused bug collecting to creating Pokémon illustrates how individual passions can lead to significant contributions that benefit society as a whole. By embracing a strength-based approach and celebrating diversity, teachers create inclusive learning environments where all students feel accepted and respected.

2. Presume Competence

Let's always presume competence in our students. Each child has the potential to think, learn, and understand the world around them. Instead of underestimating their abilities, let's provide the necessary support and tools for their success. Believing in the competence of each student doesn't mean ignoring the existence of their disabilities. Instead, it's about recognizing that learning and growth are always possible. Our goal as teachers is to support every student by seeing beyond the disability and focusing on the potential within.

> "Even if they look like they're not paying attention, they may be! This is especially true for non-speaking students: we need to presume competence and understanding."
>
> Maddie Fry

Additionally, we acknowledge that not everyone communicates through speech. Some individuals may use Augmentative and Alternative Communication (AAC) such as sign language or speech-generating devices (See "Introducing Communication," pg. 174,). We need to honor these forms of communication and provide tools for our students to learn how to use them effectively. This allows our students to have a voice and express themselves in ways that feel comfortable and natural for them. Whether speaking, signing, using AAC devices, writing, gestures, or pantomime, honoring their unique ways of expression can boost their self-assurance and eagerness to engage. Validating all forms of communication not only helps students who face challenges with traditional methods but also fosters a classroom environment that values diversity and respect. This compassionate approach cultivates an inclusive learning space where every student feels understood and appreciated for their voice.

> "I want teachers to know that just because I process things differently, it doesn't mean that I am not capable."
>
> Denis Yudin

3. Accommodate Diverse Needs

In today's classrooms, creating an inclusive learning environment is essential, particularly for neurodivergent students, as small adjustments can significantly impact their educational experience. Providing sensory-friendly spaces and supports, such as quiet corners, noise-canceling headphones, and dimmed lighting, helps students regulate sensory experiences and manage potential overload. Classwide sensory-friendly strategies benefit all students and prevents anyone from feeling singled out.

Flexibility in seating arrangements is another critical aspect, including allowing various seating options and allowing for and accommodating movements like stimming or wiggling during academic periods. Incorporating textures under desks for sensory input and allowing minor behaviors like twirling pens or walking around can create a more supportive learning environment. Rather than viewing certain behaviors as noncompliant or disruptive, it's essential to recognize that students may be meeting their own sensory needs to stay focused. In a truly flexible seating environment, students have the agency to choose their seats, promoting comfort and engagement.

Visual supports play a crucial role in aiding understanding and communication. Beyond traditional posters, incorporating visual cues like colored circles for seating arrangements or using appropriate timers and visuals tailored to students' levels can enhance comprehension and engagement. Collaborating with service providers can help identify the most effective visual strategies for individual students. Designating spaces for whole group, small group, and independent work, as well as incorporating analog timers to help students internalize the concept of time, fosters predictability and reduces overwhelm.

"We need to break the idea of what a 'good classroom' looks like with all students sitting still, looking forward toward the teacher, or quietly and calmly working independently. Instead, we need to recognize that attending and engaging looks different across different students, and we need to allow self-regulation."

Kristen Morrison

4. Foster an Accepting Classroom Culture

Fostering an inclusive classroom culture is crucial for the development and success of all students, neurodiverse and neurotypical. By celebrating and normalizing differences, teachers create environments where every student feels included. Here are some actionable ways you can promote acceptance in your classroom:

- Incorporate books about neurodiverse students into your curriculum and classroom libraries to celebrate and normalize differences.
- Allow students to make choices within the classroom, creating natural opportunities for them to see the diversity of choices made by their peers and recognize and appreciate differences.
- Contribute to an accepting culture by celebrating events like Down Syndrome and Autism Acceptance Month, and advocating for these to be celebrated schoolwide.
- Emphasize the importance of understanding diverse needs and perspectives by teaching students that "different friends need different things in different ways."
- Recognize and celebrate the achievements of both neurotypical and neurodiverse students, fostering a sense of inclusivity and belonging for all.
- Implement strategies and accommodations beneficial for neurodivergent students, which often benefit neurotypical students as well, promoting universal inclusivity.
- Reassure students facing concerns about fairness by emphasizing that everyone is doing their best, responding with empathy and understanding, thus fostering an environment where all students feel valued and supported.

> "At an early age, students view themselves as a 'good learner' or 'successful in school' or not, and this is often shaped by teachers. This impacts their self-esteem as an adult."
>
> Arielle Starkman

5. Use Inclusive Instructions

Inclusive instructions are essential for teachers to meet the diverse needs of all students in the classroom. Inclusivity promotes equity, fosters belonging, and maximizes each student's potential, leading to more positive academic outcomes.

Try these adaptations to make your instructions more inclusive of all students' diverse needs:

- Utilize materials that your students are interested in, such as incorporating digital planners, to-do lists, and reminders for students interested in electronics. For visual learners, allow students to write or brainstorm on their desks with dry-erase markers.
- Offer diverse learning stations such as one-on-one sessions with the teacher, independent desks for focused work, hands-on activities, and reading-/auditory-based tasks to cater to different learning styles.
- Establish a folder system for independent work periods, allowing students to choose tasks throughout the week and the order in which they complete the assignments. This can help promote autonomy and time management skills.
- Encourage students to explore their hyperfocus and special interests. For instance, if a student is passionate about rocket ships but struggles with standard reading assignments, provide reading materials about rocket ships or encourage them to find related reading materials independently.
- Deliver clear and specific instructions, avoiding overwhelming students with multiple steps at once. Utilize multi-modal approaches, including real images alongside text instructions, to enhance comprehension.
- Provide visual checklists for common routine tasks like cleaning up desks to guide neurodiverse students and reduce anxiety. These supports are especially helpful at the beginning of the school year and after breaks.
- Reassure students facing concerns about fairness by emphasizing that everyone is doing their best, and it's okay that everyone's best looks different

A Note From Morgan:

During my time as a co-teacher in a 4th grade Autism classroom, we had a curriculum standard that required students to demonstrate knowledge of the plot, characters, and other elements of a story. The standard was something along the lines of: "Describe in depth a character, setting, or event in a story or drama, drawing on specific details in the text (e.g., a character's thoughts, words, or actions)."

Instead of assigning a traditional book report to meet this standard, we took a different approach. After reading aloud A Wrinkle in Time, our lead teacher, Ms. Mesa Whitt, gave the students the freedom to choose how they wanted to demonstrate their understanding of the book's characters, setting, and plot. With 12 students in the class, each one chose a different type of project: one student constructed an entire world on Minecraft replicating scenes from the book with incredible detail, another taught themselves to code and programmed two characters exchanging dialogue from the book, and two students collaborated on an alternate reality story set on a different planet, but with the same characters, and drew illustrated scenes from the actual book, as well as their own alternate reality. We even had their new book printed and bound, which excitedly asked to read aloud to the class.

It's important to note that all of the students in this class had struggled in previous school placements. Upon arriving at our school, the Anova Center of Education, they brought with them a history of distrust toward teachers, and many had experienced bullying. Additionally, several had records of disciplinary actions and suspensions due to challenging behaviors. However, by granting these students the autonomy to choose how they approached the task, they flourished. We dedicated one hour each day to working on this project, and many of them chose to continue working on it during their free time. By the end of the project, it was clear they were proud of what they had accomplished. It was an unforgettable experience for me. Purely by coincidence, Garrett Winters, one of the autistic self-advocates who collaborated on this book, is a graduate of the Anova Center for Education and still proudly wears his school bracelet.

6. Embody a Relationship-First Approach

Before starting to teach, especially skills that may be more difficult, we have to have a positive, supportive relationship with our students. We want to build relationships with our students where they feel like they can be themselves and not be judged or have to hide who they really are.

Masking, in the context of neurodiversity, refers to the conscious or unconscious efforts of individuals to hide or suppress their neurological differences to blend in or appear more neurotypical. This can involve mimicking social interactions, hiding stimming behaviors, or suppressing traits that might be deemed unconventional or unacceptable in certain environments like a school setting. Masking requires a significant emotional and cognitive toll on the individual, as it not only conceals their true identity but also can lead to feelings of isolation, exhaustion, and decreased self-esteem. It's a survival mechanism many in the neurodivergent community adopt, often from a young age, in response to societal pressures and stigmatization. Understanding and recognizing the signs of masking is crucial for creating supportive and inclusive spaces that allow individuals to express themselves and build stronger student and teacher relationships.

"Masking is not exclusive to Autism, but many autistics have experienced this. It's like trying to fit into a 'normal.' It's a double identity, putting on a persona or an act. We watch how other people are acting and trying to do the same. This is trying to conceal or downplay having Autism. This is different than when I feel comfortable. It's exhausting."

Denis Yudin

The impact of masking on academic performance cannot be overstated. When students feel pressured to hide their true selves, their focus shifts from learning to conforming. This not only stifles their creativity but can significantly impede their cognitive and emotional development. Children and adolescents constantly navigating the complexities of their identity may experience increased anxiety and stress, leading to a noticeable decline in motivation, engagement, and, ultimately, academic achievement.

"Teachers should foster an environment where they feel comfortable and safe to drop their mask. It doesn't mean letting them do whatever they want; it's about letting them just 'be' without drawing so much attention to it and overcompensating. In a chill and calm way, enforcing that equality."

Denis Yudin

Our approach is centered around building strong relationships with our students and their families. We welcome students' differences and neuordiversities with understanding and acceptance. Effective teaching flourishes when there is a collaborative bond among our students, their families, and us as educators. Each party plays a vital role. (See "Establishing a Positive Classroom Culture," pg. 50 and "Building Rapport," pg. 106).

7. Prioritize Emotional Regulation

Emphasizing emotional regulation over compliance is key. Rather than enforcing strict compliance, we guide our students in managing their emotions by providing a supportive environment. We utilize a "Firm, but Flexible" approach (See page 186). When faced with resistance, adjust the activity to support their needs and foster self-advocacy skills. Create a safe space where students can openly share their feelings without fear of judgment. It's essential to embed emotional literacy into the everyday curriculum, teaching students that feeling a wide range of emotions is a part of life and that expressing these feelings is healthy and encouraged. Offer alternatives for emotional expression, such as journals, emotion wheels, or "feeling check-ins" at the beginning or end of the day. Such practices help students understand and articulate their emotions, fostering a compassionate classroom atmosphere.

> "Starting the day by checking in with your students can be incredibly meaningful."
>
> Michelle Vinokurov, autistic self-advocate

Morning check-ins not only set the tone for the day with genuine connections but also enable proactive addressing of any issues they may be facing, supporting them through emotional regulation skills before introducing academic content. This simple act of care and attention can be carried out through a classwide morning meeting or a one-on-one session with specific students. Emotional-regulation strategies should also be taught throughout the day, whether through structured teaching or through natural teaching moments. (See "Modeling" pg. 154 and "Self-Regulation" pg. 172). These are skills that need to be taught and practiced, just like academics. And also like academics, some students may need more support than others.

Amplifying Neurodiverse Voices

To provide further insights into how teachers can support students with diverse needs, we believe it's essential to amplify their voices. In the following pages, you'll hear directly from individuals with neurodivergent perspectives. First, Garrett Winters shares his reflections on a teaching methodology tailored to support students with ADHD, as published by Silvia Pokrivčáková and colleagues in 2015. Garrett himself is aspiring to become a teacher. Following Garrett's insights, we've featured an interview with Carver McDonald. Carver, who is Morgan's cousin, proudly shares his journey as a young adult with Down Syndrome who is loving life!

Introduction

"Hey! My name is Garrett Winters, and I'm a gay nonbinary autistic activist with ADHD. I have a Bachelor's in English Education and am currently getting my Masters in Teaching English to Speakers of Other Languages at the American College of Greece in Athens. I made this as a handout to give to my classmates as part of a presentation because the methodology is very well thought-out, and I wanted to give my insider perspective on why it works from an AuDHD (Autistic and ADHD) viewpoint as it works for both neurodivergences.

The FIRST methodology, as described by Silvia Pokrivčáková and colleagues in their 2015 publication, provides a framework for teaching students with ADHD. For each letter in FIRST, you will find a quoted explanation of the teaching methodology, followed by my perspective on its effectiveness."

F: Fun

The education process for ADHD learners should comprise 1) good management and organization, and 2) elements of fun and novelty. This means that some education activities are realized through games or competitions, though the teacher insists on predefined rules. As these learners have problems with concentration, motivation, and impulsivity, an external reward serves as a stimulus for their work.

"Our minds aren't great at producing dopamine (the chemical that your brain produces when you accomplish something) so having some form of external reward will help encourage focus. A great method (and one that I use for myself with apps that I use to focus and keep track of things) is gamification; turning things into games helps activate the hyperfocus. Pretty much any activity can be a game when you set a time limit on it with a reward if it gets done within a certain time frame; this lets us compete with the clock and ourselves instead of with other students."

I: Individualism

This sub-principle draws on the fact that all children are individual human beings with individual interests and opinions. ADHD children are no exception. Carter R. C. (2011) writes that the diagnosis of ADHD children is often perceived as more important than the individuality and personality beneath the surface of the disorder. This may result in underestimating and lowering their self-confidence.

"Rejection Sensitive Dysphoria (a very common symptom of ADHD) largely stems from being expected to hold to neurotypical standards and failing consistently—this makes it so focusing on the positive with your ADHD students and rewarding them for their unique strengths will help a lot. Interactive activities are a great way to let us shine and keep us engaged."

R: Rules

Rules can be defined as general standards for learners' behavior in all classroom situations (Wayne State University, n.d.). They are beneficial both for the teacher, as a tool for effective classroom management, and the ADHD or ADD children, as they provide a safe environment for them to express their personalities.

"Help your autistic and ADHD students by making your expectations incredibly clear and unambiguous (including things that you might expect your students to already know), consistently visible (for instance, on a poster next to the whiteboard; having them in a place where we can easily go back to makes it so forgetting isn't as easy), and in the form of positive statements ("Listen when someone else is talking" instead of "No talking out of turn" is the example she gives; this does help as you're giving a concrete guideline that we need to follow instead of a thing not to do). Presentations like a traffic light where a red light means no talking, orange indicates low-level talking allowed, and green indicates open talking, could also be useful."

S: Simplicity

The fourth step of the FIRST methodology is closely connected to the previous steps. It is relevant not only for rules in the EFL classroom but also for teacher language and task instructions. All instructions should be as simple and concrete as possible. According to the U.S. Department of Education (2008), "the simpler the expectations communicated to an ADHD student, the more likely it is that he or she will comprehend and complete them in a timely and productive manner." If a task comprises several sub-tasks, instructions should be provided one by one. This procedure helps the ADHD learners to maintain the focus on a concrete issue.

"Not leaving anything to interpretation and having everything spelled out is very important, as is not overloading students with too many instructions (hence the part about providing subtasks one by one instead of all at once)."

T: Time Management

One difference between ADHD children and their classmates is their difficulty in changing between activities. If these children are happy with an activity in which they have been involved, it can take some time to focus their attention on something else. For example, after a dynamic role-play, reading or listening activities can struggle to engage their attention. Therefore, it is necessary to plan activities beforehand and to inform children about the course of the lesson.

"To continue with everything spelled out, having an outline of the day (with what time things will be labeled, if possible) will help ADHD/autistic students a lot. Having a clock is also a good idea, as it provides a visual reminder of how long things are.

Beyond the methodology, I also have a few tips.

First off, please be patient. We are trying.

We can get distracted and take longer on things, need a lot of reminders, and it may be hard for you, but... try being us. We know that we need to do things and are in a constant war in our own heads because of it, trying to focus despite our neurochemistry working against us. That part really sucks, and it leads to a lot of internalized ableism and self-hate, fed by every negative reaction that we get which stays in our heads as proof that we are somehow bad. You can help your students fight that by not making a huge deal and working to cheer their spirits any time they do something good—or you can be a voice of negativity that will possibly last for the rest of their lives.

Second, can't stress enough that the most important thing is clarity of expectations in all forms; knowing specifics of what is needed helps us cling to them and follow them, but not having them leads to a form of paralysis because our minds don't know what to do. Have them written and accessible to students so they can refer to them as they go on as opposed to forgetting them, and spell all the details out even if there are things that you'd expect students to get without them being stated."

Reference: Pokrivčáková, S., et al. (2015). *Teaching Foreign Languages to Learners with Special Educational Needs: e-textbook for foreign language teachers* (pp. 83-90). Nitra: Constantine the Philosopher University.

An Interview with Carver McDonald

Morgan: Hey Carver! Tell me a little about yourself. What do you like to do?

Carver: Hi! I'm Carver McDonald. I'm 19 years old and I'm in the 18+ program at my high school. I like to make my parents happy and have so much with them. I also like to watch TV. I'm a fan of guitars. My favorite color is purple, and I love girls!

Morgan: I know you graduated from high school last year—congratulations! What was the highlight of your senior year?

Carver: There was actually a lot of great things! One of the best parts was being in an article in my local newspaper! The article was about me and my Instagram, where I talk about going on social outings and interviewing people. My family friend Amy Wilson helps me with this! (Check it out at @xtra_with_carver) I also loved graduation because that was a time I got to spend with a lot of my friends. It was so inspiring.

Morgan: So cool! And what are you doing now?

Carver: I have a paid job at H-E-B Center, and I've done pretty well with filling the condiments like ketchup, ranch, mustard, pickles—I love pickles! I'm also in the 18+ program where I take classes and do social outings, which means that I get to go places like restaurants. Right now, I'm taking a class on dating skills and a dancing class!

Morgan: What programs did your high school offer that celebrated your strengths and interests?

Carver: One thing is that I was Homecoming King! I also really liked the opportunity to work with one of the teachers, and I liked them. They are funny and inspiring. I think it'd be a dream job to be a teacher. I also had a really cool class called Broadcast. I got to be an anchor working with a reporter and interview people at my school on the school news. This was an opportunity for me to overcome my fears.

Morgan: Can you share a time when you felt really happy at school?

Carver: I feel that I'm really good at helping people with broken hearts. I was there for them, and they liked that. That made me feel like I'm a good friend to my friends at school.

Morgan: Why do you think it's important for schools to make sure everyone feels welcomed and included?

Carver: Because that is the way to go from a darkness to a light of love! And everyone should feel loved!

Morgan: Can you share some examples of how your teachers have helped you be successful at school?

Carver: My teachers helped me do my affirmations and learn to stand up for myself. I learned to talk about what is happening and I learned social skills. I feel that I'm happy and included with other students who are like me.

Morgan: What advice would you give to a teacher who wants to be better at helping students with disabilities?

Carver: Remember you never know what other students have gone through. If you see a student crying or they have a problem, help them. Do everything with a reason; do it for them. Also, we should remember that teachers are all different, just like everyone is different! Being different is good!

Morgan: Are there any special quotes you like to live by and want to share with us?

Carver: We rise by lifting others! This describes the true meaning of a good community.

Promoting "Happy, Relaxed, and Engaged"

Dr. Greg Hanley, in his paper "A Perspective on Today's ABA," emphasizes that individuals with Autism learn best when they feel joy. To create an environment where students feel happy, relaxed, and engaged while learning, teachers can have conversations with them about their likes and dislikes. This cultivates feelings of security and empowerment, which allows students to reach an ideal condition for learning and developing acceptance, tolerance, and cooperation skills.

Happy

To promote happiness, teachers can learn proactively about what brings their students joy, offer more autonomy in student choices throughout the day, and implement individualized rewards tailored to individual student needs. A happy environment is where students are comfortable and eager to learn, leading to increased attention and engagement in the academic activities.

Relaxed

A relaxed student is someone who is calm and free of current distress. It is essential to recognize that relaxation can look different from person to person. Some students may be relaxed while engaging in self-stimulatory behaviors like pacing around or flapping their hands. Teachers should create a safe and supportive space where students can be themselves. Strategies to promote student relaxation can be different for each student but may include incorporating calming activities such as deep breathing exercises or listening to soft music with dimmed lights. Additionally, allowing students to take breaks when needed and providing a comfortable space for them to decompress can also contribute to a relaxed atmosphere in the classroom.

Engaged

True engagement entails helping students actively participate in learning activities rather than being passive observers. It's crucial to recognize when a student is genuinely interacting with the content, rather than just looking at it or going through the motions without genuinely being interested. Strategies to promote engagement include individualizing materials based on preferences and interests, offering choices in how students can engage with the content, and increasing opportunities to respond (OTRs). By promoting active engagement, students are more likely to retain information and develop a deeper understanding of and connection to the material.

Importance of "Happy, Relaxed, and Engaged"

Dr. Hanley emphasizes that when students are "happy, relaxed, and engaged," teachers convey acknowledgment, visibility, and support, reducing the likelihood of challenging behaviors. A classwide approach could be dedicating the first five to ten minutes of each day to allowing students to meet their individual needs, whether through sensory activities, social interactions, or personal reflection. This proactive approach sets a positive tone for the day and supports the well-being and engagement of all students.

Establishing a Positive Classroom Culture

The Power of Positivity

Think back to the last time someone gave you a compliment. How did it make you feel? Words hold immense power, especially within the walls of a classroom. Research shows that giving positive praise five times more than redirections leads to higher rates of student participation, improved academic outcomes, reduced rates of disruptive behaviors, more student confidence, and better student-teacher relationships. This is called the 5:1 ratio. With this ratio it allows every student to experience positive reinforcement. But how do we embed this ratio into the daily rhythm of our classrooms?

The goal isn't to shower empty praises and say "good job" over and over again to every single student. It's about being specific and genuine. It's about noticing and validating the effort it takes to wait patiently or to complete a task you knew was going to be challenging for your student. Behavior-specific praise helps both you, as the teacher and your students focus on positive behaviors and actions. It is one of the most powerful tools teachers have in their repertoire. It also decreases inappropriate and challenging behaviors and, therefore, reduces the need for corrections. Finally, it not only helps build your student's self-esteem and self-control, but at the end of the day, YOU feel better! Think about days when you feel like all you did was redirect your students all day versus days when you incorporated more positive and behavior-specific praise. It makes everyone feel better!

Of course, there will be days when maintaining this golden 5:1 ratio feels like an uphill battle. We know that every classroom has its dynamics, with some students requiring more guidance than others. The goal is not perfection but to create an overall positive classroom environment where students hear more praise than correction. To help this feel more doable for your classroom, share this page with your paraprofessionals and other support staff. It's not all on you! Their positive praise for students counts towards the 5:1 ratio as well!

Positive Greetings at the Door and Pre-Correction

Have you ever experienced this? You are walking down the hallway and see a colleague and say "good morning," only to be met with silence as they walk on by. It can leave you feeling deflated and uneasy, right? Starting your day off on the wrong foot can set a negative tone for the rest of the day. This is the same with your students. A positive greeting at the door in the morning can change the outcome of their day. That's why it's crucial to make an effort to greet your students at the door each morning. Those few seconds of connection can impact not only your entire day but even shape the course of the school year (research shows this!).

A recent study showed that an act as simple as giving personalized greetings to each student at the start of the day led to a 20% increase in academic engagement time and a 10% decrease in disruptive behaviors. This shows how this zero-cost, low-effort strategy can improve expected behaviors without giving any office referrals or detentions. We even have a Greetings at the Door Poster for you in the Tools chapter!

When greeting students, it's important to utilize various approaches to create a positive and welcoming classroom atmosphere. This can involve using their name, making eye contact if they are comfortable, and offering friendly nonverbal gestures like handshakes, high-fives, or thumbs-up signs. Additionally, providing a few words of encouragement and directing them to the first activity can help set a positive tone for the day - this is known as giving a pre-correction. These gentle reminders can remind students of expectations as they enter the classroom.

When teaching and practicing greetings, approach it with the same dedication as any other crucial classroom routine. Offering students choices in how they are greeted helps ensure they feel comfortable and valued. Visual aids can aid students in understanding their options and making selections more easily. It's also beneficial to observe students' moods and reactions as they enter the classroom, using this opportunity to connect with and support those who may need it.

When classroom behavior management strategies rely heavily on reprimands, research shows that it leads to stress for both teachers and students. This stress manifests in various ways, including an increase in disruptive behaviors, higher levels of emotional exhaustion among teachers, and a rise in rates of off-task behavior. Shifting from a reactionary, disciplinary approach to a proactive, rewarding approach creates a positive classroom climate.

Supporting Paraprofessionals

Note from Janna: Some of the most remarkable individuals who have profoundly influenced me have undoubtedly been classroom paraprofessionals. As a young teacher, I've been fortunate to collaborate with paraprofessionals who bring years of invaluable experience to the classroom. They've shared insights into behavior management, classroom dynamics, school routines, and procedures. Not only do they foster strong relationships with school staff like the librarians, custodians, office managers, speech pathologists, other service providers, and teaching staff, but they also possess a deep understanding of school intricacies.

> Some of my greatest mentors and teachers
> have been my classroom paraprofessionals.

Paraprofessionals, known by various titles like teacher assistants, instructional aides, paras, and paraeducators, hold a crucial position in schools. They provide valuable classroom support to students under the guidance of licensed teachers, offering additional assistance to enhance student learning.

As teachers, we know how important paraprofessionals are in helping us support our students with diverse needs. These dedicated individuals can make or break your classroom. They play a crucial role in the classroom, providing one-on-one assistance, implementing behavior plans, and ensuring every student has access to a quality education. Research shows that more than 75% of school-based paraprofessionals encounter challenging student behavior on a daily or weekly basis, spending over 20% of their day addressing these behaviors. With this in mind, it is essential to establish clear expectations and roles to help paraprofessionals feel more prepared and supported. Sit down with each paraprofessional individually to discuss their responsibilities, goals, and any specific student needs they should be aware of. Then, describe what they can expect from you as their classroom teacher and lead supervisor. By setting clear co-expectations from the start, you can ensure everyone is on the same page and working toward common objectives.

Balancing the support of a classroom full of students can be difficult for a teacher. This is where paraprofessional support is everything! Provide regular training opportunities for paraprofessionals to enhance their skills and knowledge. We understand this can feel like a challenge when most paraprofessionals' hours are allotted for times they are actively supporting students.

8 Tips for Finding Time for Paraprofessional Training:

1. Schedule Mini-Training Sessions

Could you commit to five minutes at the start or end of the day? It can be as simple as a quick check-in to focus on a specific skill or challenge that has popped up. This micro-training approach can help keep paraprofessionals engaged and motivated without taking up too much time.

2. Co-Teach to Demonstrate Best Practices

Your paraprofessionals can learn so much from seeing you in action. Take a moment to co-teach a lesson, showcasing techniques and strategies that can support students. It's important to do a think-aloud where you are sharing why you are doing what you are doing in the moment. For example, you could add explanations when speaking aloud to the whole class, "I'm setting the Time Timer for 20 minutes so everyone can see how long we're doing independent reading." Or directly to the paraprofessional, "These students have reading accommodations, so I'm highlighting the instructions for them in their reading packets."

3. Utilize "Teachable Moments"

During your school day, organic moments arise that can serve as impromptu training. Take a quick moment to share what went well in that moment and what they could change the next time. Encourage your paraprofessionals to reflect on these experiences with you, fostering growth together through daily interactions.

4. Empower Through Peer Observations

Do you have an established paraprofessional excelling in an area where your new paraprofessional could grow? Create in-the-moment teaching opportunities by pointing out specific skills that the other paraprofessional is doing well. Either in the moment or after school, describe and explain the actionable steps that they did and why it was effective. Connecting the teaching to a rationale can help! For example, "We know that this student struggles with getting off the computer. To prepare for that, she first gave him a countdown timer (Priming); then when he asked if he could have more time, she said, 'Yes, during the next break,' using the Better Way to Say 'No' strategy. When he listened to the instruction, she immediately recognized this by giving him praise and a star on his token board." This peer modeling approach fosters an atmosphere where all staff are acknowledged for their strengths and shared learning is not just encouraged, but celebrated.

5. Create a Resource Corner

Allocate a space in your classroom where resources like articles, books, and guides are readily available for your paraprofessionals to explore during downtime. Maybe you have a few students absent, or there is an assembly, so there are a few rare minutes of downtime. Have some resources available for staff to look at. This might spark some creative ideas, interventions, or renewed excitement toward trying something new. This guidebook, for example, would be a great resource for your resource corner!

6. Online Professional Development

There are countless online resources available for professional development. Encourage your paraprofessionals to take advantage of these resources. This could be through webinars, virtual conferences, or even self-paced courses. Not only does this save time on scheduling in-person training, but it also allows for more flexibility and personalized learning opportunities.

7. Provide Feedback and Encouragement

Just like our students enjoy hearing our positive praise, make it a point to provide ongoing recognition and feedback to your paraprofessionals, delivering it with kindness and constructive intent. Sharing positive praise helps to acknowledge our paraprofessionals' strengths, work efforts, commitment, and dedication. Show them that you are grateful for them, their efforts, and their impact on student learning.

8. Promote Communication and Collaboration

Encourage open communication and regular collaboration meetings where paraprofessionals can voice concerns, share ideas, and actively participate in the planning process. Communication is key for any strong team. By working together as a cohesive team toward common goals, everyone can feel supported and motivated to do their best for the students.

An Interview with a Paraprofessional

Leslie Sanders is a dedicated and compassionate paraprofessional with over 16 years of experience in the field. She brings a wealth of knowledge and expertise to her role. Currently, she is in a preschool through kindergarten Special Day Class (SDC), where she continues to make a positive impact on the lives of her students.

Ms. Leslie has worked with Janna Bedoyan, the co-author of this book, for over ten years. Colleagues and parents alike have praised Leslie for her dedication and unwavering commitment to her students' growth. With a natural ability to connect with and support her students, Ms. Leslie's passion for helping our youngest students shines through in everything she does. When she enters the classroom in the morning, all the students smile and greet her with the same level of excitement that she brings every day. Whether creating lesson plans, taking data, doing amazing art projects, or providing individualized support, she makes it all look easy. Ms. Leslie's dedication to her students' growth is unwavering. She truly embodies what it means to be an exceptional paraprofessional.

Morgan: Hi Ms. Leslie! Tell us a little about yourself.

Leslie: Hello! So, I'm a mom; I'm a grandma. I've worked at Fresno Unified since 2008. I started as a sub and have worked in afterschool programs, special education, functional skills programs—a lot of settings! I've enjoyed that because there's been so much variety in the types of students I've worked with. When I was assigned to support my first autistic student, to be honest, I was nervous, I was scared, because I was like, I don't know this. I don't want to do this. I don't know what I'm supposed to do. But I quickly realized that I really liked it! It was like, my niche. My supervisor was like, you have the energy. Just be natural. Just be natural. And I'm like, okay. So then after that, it felt really easy! At the end of the year working with my student, she got invited to go in the limo with all the other kids for their 6th grade graduation, and it was really exciting to see her be included like that. So that's when I knew that this was where I belonged. I love it so much.

Morgan: I imagine it was so rewarding to see the student you've been working with enjoy this very special moment with her peers.

Leslie: Yes! To me, it's like the biggest thing in the world. Just like today, I made a shirt for one of our students. It's his favorite book, and I made it for him, and he loved it so much. It made his day. I was so happy. Those are the little things that make me love my job so much more. I love those little milestones.

Morgan: I know that you're also really crafty. So another reason why you're made to be in the classroom!

Leslie: Yes, I have this passion for working with students, specifically autistic students, and now I feel like I have my home in my job. And that's what I say. I say that that's my home. When I first interviewed with Janna, I said, all I'm really looking for is a home. And I meant, like, as a home, that's where I'm going to stay till it's time to retire. And in that amount of time that we've been together, it has become like a home because we spend so much time there together with these little guys and talking to their families, and it does become like a home. Like a family. And I love that.

Morgan: So how long have you and Janna been working together?

Leslie: We've been together since 2014. So this is our tenth year together. Wow.

Morgan: Ten year anniversary! Exciting! Could you share a little more about what your day-to-day role looks like as a paraprofessional in this classroom?

Leslie: Well, for the most part, we just know what to do. This is my area. This is your area. This is my student. This is your student. And so we kind of split that up between all of us. Janna takes care of leading the whole group lessons and we take care of supporting particular students.

Morgan: How many paras are there?

Leslie: There's five adults in the class altogether. One teacher, four paras, and 11 students, at least right now. We work a lot together. If one of us is having a hard time, then Janna or another of us will go over and support. Wherever the little fire is, we all help in putting it out.

Morgan: So much teamwork! And I also know that there's a lot of AAC happening in your classroom, but not all the students are nonvocal. So can you share how you all, as a team, are really creating that inclusive classroom for your students?

We try to make the whole day inclusive for everyone.

Leslie: We try to make the whole day inclusive for everyone. We incorporate it in every circle time. We usually have a few students that are very good at it, and we let them take turns controlling the device. They can run it better than us sometimes!

Actually, when I first started with AAC, I was like, "I'm never going to get this. I can't do it. I'm too old haha." But now I've learned the different languages! Actually, I'm more fluent in LAMP. So when we're doing it, one student will be on one side using Proloquo, another one over here with LAMP, and then the students that don't have a device, they just sing along and watch. At stations, we have laminated core boards for all students so they can get a little help if they need it. Even if our students start talking, we still encourage the AAC device to always be there because sometimes they can't get the right word. Whether vocal student or nonvocal student, there's always that access to communication nearby them.

> *Whether vocal student or nonvocal student, there's always that access to communication nearby them.*

Morgan: You mentioned you're more fluent with LAMP. Can you explain what that means?

Leslie: In our classroom, we all know which AAC language is most intuitive for us. That way, when we're working with the students and if one is struggling with LAMP, I can jump in because it's easier for me. There are staff who are naturally better at Proloquo2go and they can help with those or model those languages. I think that's a really good way of using the different strengths that each paraprofessional can bring to the classroom.

Morgan: Was it also hard or intimidating for you to learn behavior strategies, or did that come more naturally to you?

Leslie: No, not at all. I feel like that comes to me naturally. Sometimes when we were in class, there's like some that stump me, but it'll take me a little bit. And I'm like, okay, let me think about it. Let me think about it. What strategy can I use? How can I help them? And I feel like to me, behavior

is a strength for me because I usually get success. And so I love that. It makes me happy. And for the little students, for them to feel like, "Okay, if it's hard for me, I know there's somebody to help me," I think that makes them feel like it's not going to be that big a deal.

Morgan: Do you have tips for paraprofessionals who do struggle with learning behavior strategies?

Leslie: A lot of it has to do with how you carry yourself. I can just come in and be calm and be excited to be there for my students because I love my job. So I'm showing up to work with a big smile on my face.

Morgan: That's actually really important! You're creating a classroom of joy where students can also look forward to coming each day. And because they know you're there for them, they probably feel like they can trust you.

What recommendations would you give to other teacher and para teams that don't feel like they're working together seamlessly?

Leslie: Each person has a strength that they can bring to the team, and I think everyone needs to acknowledge that. Like, this person brings this, that person brings that. It's all about finding everyone's strengths. I also think having that communication where the teacher sets that tone of being able to feel really like it's open and share your ideas and share what you're good at and that it's listened to.

Morgan: Do you have structured times where you can share ideas with your teacher?

Leslie: Once a month we will sit down and we'll talk about behaviors that have happened. We talk about who calmed the behavior and how they did it. We need to know so that if it worked, we all do that same approach as a team. We also do a lot of brainstorming about behaviors and planning on how to respond.

Morgan: How do you decide which strategies or approach to go with?

Leslie: We ask everyone, "What do you think? What would you have done? And we never put down anyone's answers. Everybody's input means something. Everybody has a different relationship and understanding of each student, and that's important. The whole team giving their input has value. I think that means a lot. Being able to trust each other is key. So I think that trust and communication will make everything more successful.

Morgan: What else do you collaborate on during these monthly brainstorm sessions?

Leslie: Usually, Janna will read over any new IEP goals, and she'll say, "Okay, here's the goal…" and we'll all brainstorm where we can work on it. And not just where we can work on it, but how we will work on it. Everybody puts in their input.

Morgan: I love that. So you're deciding as a team how you can all work on the goal throughout activities that are already scheduled for this student.

Each person has a strength that they can bring to the team, and I think everyone needs to acknowledge that. Like, this person brings this, that person brings that. It's all about finding everyone's strengths.

Leslie: Yes. And not only during the activity, but how are you going to do it? How are you going to set that up? How are you going to teach them? Because in each activity, the skill can look completely different. With this approach, it's been easier for us to help students accomplish their goals. We actually just started doing this as a whole team, and a lot of our students' progress reports are already showing goals met!

Morgan: What advice would you give to a paraprofessional who's new to the field? They want to do a great job and help their students, but they haven't really developed the skill set yet. What advice would you suggest for them and their classroom teacher?

Leslie: I say enhance the positive, girl. Enhance the positive. If they cleaned the table after an activity, "Great job!" They did something out of the ordinary, "Great job!" It's all about recognizing their efforts. And for them, knowing who to ask for help. Even if they're afraid to ask, ask. And the other staff should be like, "I'll show you. We'll do it together." And that's a big thing. Making someone feel welcomed right away. Making them feel like it's okay to ask questions.

Morgan: I'm sure that your district does some training during onboarding, but how are you and Janna helping to train new staff in the classroom?

Leslie: So we like to start out small. We don't give them a big responsibility straight from the gate. For example, "You're going to record the words. If the student says a word, you record it." So just one task. And then the next time it was something bigger. It's slowly building up so they feel confident and really learned the skill. But it's also about finding their strengths right away. Sometimes I watch our other coworkers and see little things. I'm like, "I didn't even think of that!" That's the best thing about getting to work with other people is really learning all the time from each other.

Morgan: What advice would you give to teachers on how they can they recognize and acknowledge their paraprofessionals?

Leslie: A lot of people are motivated by different things. So, I think that the teacher might need to take that extra step to be like, okay, well, let me get to know a little bit about you and what is important to you.

Morgan: What are ways that teachers can make their paraprofessionals feel valued and appreciated?

Leslie: Well, mine does a really good job. I'll brag about her haha. So my teacher, absolutely fabulous. She'll write notes. She texts me how special I am. She'll just give me little gifts, like a little card. And she does it for all of us. She'll bring a flower for each person. She'll make us breakfast. I mean, today she made everybody, like, bento boxes. Just the little thank yous. Even, like, she's brought some cough drops for the classroom, or, "Oh, I knew you were sick, so I bought this for you." Or, hey, just the little incentive gestures, little things that make you see that. Even if it's not, like, something from her own pocket. Or she's like, "Hey, let's have a potluck. I'll bring the main dish, everybody. And let's have a sit down. And let's conversate," because she wants to get to spend time with all of us because we don't get that. You know what I mean? So her even wanting to have that interaction time with all of us is really great for all of us. It makes all of us feel excited because it's like, "Oh, we're all going to sit down and eat lunch together." That's exciting.

Morgan: Just like you said, the little things make it go so far. And she's prioritizing. I think that's also the gift of time, right?

Leslie: Exactly. Also, like, when we're sick, she'll text us that she hopes we feel better. That little acknowledgment from the whole group or from our teacher is really great. It shows, like, she cares. It shows that we matter. What we're going through matters. I mean, yes, she wants us there, but she also wants us there healthy. She wants us there happy.

Morgan: Last question! What do you think are the most important factors for paraprofessionals and teachers to be able to work well together?

Leslie: Communication and feeling comfortable to share ideas. To be able to listen and hear feedback. At the end of every day, we kind of debrief with each other: Here's what I did that worked; here's what we need to focus on doing better tomorrow. We validate each other's ideas.

Everyone has value and is an important part of the team.

Embodying a Trauma-Informed Approach

Imagine yourself hiking in the wilderness when you suddenly come face-to-face with a bear. Your heart races and adrenaline surges, prompting you to confront, escape, or freeze. After narrowly escaping the encounter, imagine having to sit down immediately and complete a spelling test, trying to concentrate on word after word. Even if you typically excel in spelling, in this heightened state of stress and fear, focusing on such a task would likely feel nearly impossible.

Trauma-informed teaching begins with recognizing how trauma affects both learning and behavior. Educators adopting this approach interpret student behavior as a form of communication and reflect on their teaching methods to better accommodate students who may have experienced trauma.

Trauma can significantly impede our capacity to learn. When confronted with a threat, our bodies prioritize survival, redirecting energy from brain regions essential for learning. As a result, students impacted by trauma may display heightened distractibility, slower task completion, increased irritability or impulsivity, and may encounter challenges academically or behaviorally. It is crucial to acknowledge that while students may not be facing a threatening situation in your classroom, triggers unbeknownst to us can trigger a trauma response, further affecting their ability to effectively engage in learning.

> A trauma-informed approach to supporting students entails recognizing the widespread impact of trauma, integrating this understanding into all areas of student support, and prioritizing safety, trustworthiness, choice, collaboration, and empowerment.

Schools strive to nurture students on their educational path, fostering feelings of safety, support, and readiness for learning. However, numerous students have encountered trauma, ranging from abuse to natural disasters, which hinders academic progress. Communities with elevated rates of adverse childhood experiences (ACEs) often exhibit lower academic achievement rates. Trauma manifests in struggles with self-regulation, negative thoughts, hypervigilance, and difficulty trusting adults, which can lead to challenging behaviors like aggression or avoidance, often misinterpreted as ADHD symptoms. Students who have experienced trauma, particularly violence, are at a higher risk of emotional dysregulation, disruptive behaviors, declining academic performance, and negative remarks in their records compared to their peers. They may struggle with concentration, retaining learning, and may exhibit reckless or aggressive behavior.

Trauma-informed schools prioritize safety and build positive relationships to create a structured, predictable, and supportive environment. This empowers teachers to identify and respond to students' needs effectively, even when trauma goes unreported.

Students need to feel safe, valued, and supported within their school environment to learn effectively. Teachers are uniquely situated to identify, respond to, and be impacted by students' traumatic stress symptoms due to their central role in their students' lives and their ability to create meaningful, positive, trusting relationships at schools. By implementing small changes in the classroom to foster a sense of safety, teachers can significantly enhance traumatized students' ability to learn and thrive.

Our approach to working with all students should be centered on strategies that avoid re-traumatization, as we may not always know their history. Dr. Rajaraman has proposed the following four guidelines for embodying a trauma-informed approach:

Acknowledge the potential for trauma: Recent data suggests that 61% of adults and 45% of children have experienced at least one potentially traumatic event. This estimate is even higher for those with disabilities. With this in mind, we should look beyond the ABC data taught on the following pages and also acknowledge that lived experiences impact behaviors today. While effective, some behavior and teaching strategies may be trauma triggers (e.g. time out, extinction, physical prompting), which should be considered when selecting strategies.

Ensure safety and trust: Consider where your services take place, with whom, and how you can set this up to promote a feeling of security for your student. Always start a new relationship with the Building Rapport strategy to build trust and reliability. Ensure ongoing safety by honoring moments of withdrawal, promoting coping skills, and training the entire team on strategies for maintaining physical and emotional safety during high-intensity behaviors.

Promote choice and autonomy: Providing opportunities for our students to make choices gives them control over their daily lives. The Providing Choices strategy also allows our students to provide assent (agreement to participate), as they are choosing to join in! In fact, research shows that the more we provide choices, the more our students engage!

Emphasize skill building: As a way of empowering our students, teachers and service providers should prioritize skills and strategies that promote self-advocacy, communication, and independence skills over those that only aim to reduce challenging behaviors (such as punishment). We have visualized many skill-building strategies in the following chapters!

As you learn more about the foundations for supporting students with diverse needs and behavior strategies outlined in this book, we encourage you to look out for how we've integrated a trauma-informed approach into the applications and how you can incorporate these recommendations into your own classroom and teaching approach.

Recommended reading:
Rajaraman, A., Austin, J. L., Gover, H. C., Cammilleri, A. P., Donnelly, D. R., & Hanley, G. P. (2022). Toward trauma-informed applications of behavior analysis. *Journal of Applied Behavior Analysis,* 55(1), 40–61.

To help you develop individualized trauma-informed strategies for your student, we encourage you to set up and lead a collaborative brainstorming session with the student and the IEP team. The table on the next page can be used as a tool to learn more about the student's experience and potential ways the team can provide support. It may be beneficial to schedule monthly or quarterly collaborative meetings to update the support plan.

Trauma-Informed Support Plan Brainstorming

Questions to ask	Support plan ideas
What are situations or activities that trigger the student?	How to change the situation or activity to make the student feel more safe and calm:
What are the actions of staff that trigger the student?	How staff can avoid or limit these actions:
What is in the student's environment at school that may feel triggering to them?	How we can adjust the classroom environment to make the student feel more safe and calm:
What necessary interactions, situations, or instructions are triggering to the student?	How we can adjust these to be less triggering: How we can support the student with coping strategies during this time:

Understanding Why Challenging Behaviors Occur

A concerning trend of increasing behavioral challenges is emerging in classrooms, with both frequency and severity on the rise. Unfortunately, many teachers feel ill-equipped to address these behaviors such as bullying, protest, elopement, self-harm, aggression, and disrespectful language. Recent surveys indicate that more than 70% of teachers have observed a surge in disruptive behaviors, up from 66% in 2019. As a result, many teachers actively seek out information on how they can build better behaviors in their classrooms. While there are many books, online resources, and social media accounts that offer promising solutions, it can be confusing and overwhelming to know where to begin or which strategy is best for your particular classroom.

When considering individual students who engage in challenging behaviors, an individualized approach is best. In a behavioral approach, the first step to reducing these behaviors is to figure out why they're occurring in the first place. Our goal is to understand how we can better support the student with their needs, rather than just addressing the results. While reducing challenging behaviors is a common objective supported by behavior strategies and services, the true focus should be on empowering students to communicate and self-regulate effectively. Research proves that building these replacement skills is the most effective approach to minimizing challenging behaviors. To determine the appropriate skill to teach, we first identify the "function," or reason behind the behavior. From here, the choice of evidence-based strategies to choose from is more targeted, ultimately setting up the teacher for more likely success. We made it even easier for you by creating a visual table recommending strategies organized by function, which you can find on page 14.

Let's look at an example of a student who disrupts the classroom by frequently leaving their seat to pace around. This behavior not only impedes their learning, but also the learning of others. As seen in the following illustrations, this behavior could be occurring as an attempt to avoid tasks, gain attention from peers, or simply feeling the need to pace around. By recognizing that behaviors are purposeful, we pave the way for more effective behavior management strategies. There are four functions, or reasons, that behaviors may occur. You can remember them as "let's SEAA why a behavior is happening."

1. **Sensory** (an internal/external sensation or self-regulation)
2. **Escape** (from an instruction or aversive situation)
3. **Access** (to an item, activity, or the way something is done)
4. **Attention** (from others)

During a Functional Behavior Assessment (FBA), behavior experts analyze behavior patterns to uncover the underlying function. It's important to note that sometimes there are outside factors (setting events) influencing a behavior as well. This could include pain, medication, sleep, or other biological reasons. Thoughts and feelings also influence a person's behavior, although that is harder to track and measure. That's why it's important we try our best to understand the student from a comprehensive perspective and provide well-rounded support.

From analyzing situations where the behaviors most often occur, we can start to find patterns of common triggers and responses, which helps us understand what the student may need in those moments. With this understanding, we can start to create an individualized plan to teach skills that meet these same needs. This is called teaching a "functionally-equivalent replacement behavior." In the previous example about a student who paces around the classroom, we will need to determine: Is he gaining attention from the teacher/peers? Is he walking around the room so he can access some preferred items? Is the walking delaying or preventing him from completing an assigned task? Or is it fulfilling a sensory need for movement? In the following sets of illustrations, look at the clues that can help guide our understanding.

Clues that the behavior is Attention function

- The student was previously receiving attention from someone, and then that person stopped giving attention just before the target behavior occurred.
- The student's behavior attracted attention from peers or teachers. Remember that reprimands (e.g. "no," "don't do that") are also a form of attention.

The student receives attention by engaging in the behavior.

Here, as the student wanders around the classroom, he's joining into conversations with his peers.

Clues that the behavior is Access function

- A preferred item or activity was taken away from the student just before the target behavior occurred.
- The student was told "no," "not right now," or "wait."
- As a result of the behavior, the student was able to access a preferred item or activity.

The behavior enables the student to access a preferred item or activity.

Here, as the student wanders around the classroom, he's able to get his cell phone out of his backpack.

Clues that the behavior is Escape function

- The student was instructed to complete a task just before the target behavior occurred.
- Immediately after the target behavior, the expectation to complete a task was removed.

Engaging in the target behavior enables the student to escape or delay a non-preferred task or aversive situation.

Here, this student is walking away from his reading assignment, a task that he typically finds challenging.

Clues that the behavior is Sensory function

- The behavior does not seem to enable attention from others, avoidance, or access.
- The student engages in the behavior during various settings and activities.
- The behavior appears to be helping the student self-regulate.

Some students may engage in sensory behaviors as an expression of their emotions or a way to self-regulate. As long as these behaviors are not causing harm or impeding learning, there is no need to aim to reduce them.

The student is engaging in the behavior because it "feels good" or helps them self-regulate. Here, as the student wanders around the classroom, he's not avoiding work (he can still be listening to the teacher), getting attention from others, or accessing something. This is a clue that the behavior is occuring for sensory needs.

ABCs of Behavior

The first step in developing a plan to reduce a challenging behavior is to understand why the behavior occurs. To do this, you will need to attend to what is happening before (antecedent) and after (consequence) the behavior. You can do this by collecting "ABC data." Sometimes behaviors may feel like they're happening out of nowhere, but looking at the ABCs can help determine what's really causing them. As previously described, there may be factors we cannot see that influence behavior today. This could include factors like past trauma, amount of sleep, if medications were taken, or if the student is feeling sick. While we may not know everything that leads up to a behavior, by looking at the ABCs, we can start to see and understand patterns, and these patterns are what leads us toward a solution! Use the chart activity on the next page to help you become a behavior detective. Once you've determined the function, you're on your way to choosing strategies that can effectively support the student!

A	B	C
Antecedent Events that occur immediately before a behavior	**Behavior** An observable action	**Consequence** Events that occur immediately after a behavior

Examples

A	B	C
Teacher says, "Get out math book"	Student yells and throws book	Teacher instructs student to pick book up
Teacher says, "Clean up toys"	Student screams, "No!" and immediately drops to the floor and cries (tantrum)	Teacher helps student to clean up toys and start desk work

Instructions for ABC Chart

1. Choose one behavior to target (e.g. yelling, vocal protest, hitting, etc.). Include a description of what this behavior looks like for this student.
2. Every time this behavior occurs, fill out the chart with (A) what happened immediately prior, (B) what the behavior looked like, (C) what happened immediately afterward/how you responded.
3. Optional: Add comments with more information about what was happening at that time. Record information for at least four times the behavior occurs (can all be during one day if the behavior occurs a lot, or can be over several days if the behavior does not occur as often).

ABC Chart Example

Target Behavior: Elopement (leaving designated area without permission)

Antecedent What happened before the behavior?	Behavior Describe the behavior	Consequence What happened after the behavior?	Function
Teacher informed the class that there is a change in schedule today due to a morning assembly.	Student ran out of the classroom. Remained in hallway for eight minutes.	Paraprofessional talked to the student about why the assembly is important and attempted to redirect to coping skills.	
Instruction to line up at end of recess.	Student ran away from the playground and toward the school exit. Remained near exit door for five minutes.	Teacher continued giving the instruction to line up.	
Playing a game with a peer and lost.	Screamed at the student, threw the game pieces at them, and ran outside. Remained outside for 12 minutes.	Paraprofessional followed student as he walked around campus. Continued to provide instructions to return to class.	
Teacher put on video of a book being read aloud.	Student ran to the hallway. Remained in hallway for seven minutes.	Paraprofessional attempted to redirect to coping skills. When student saw that the video had ended, he returned to class.	

Your Turn!

Choose a specific behavior to target. Describe that behavior using observable and objective words ("Target Behavior"). Fill out the chart below for the next four times that behavior occurs.

Note: Sometimes, a consequence is also the antecedent for the next behavior.
Example: (A) Instruction to do worksheet; (B) Student yells; (C) Teacher repeats the instruction to do worksheet // (A) Teacher repeats the instruction to do worksheet; (B) Student rips paper; (C) Teacher tells student to go take a break.

You can leave the function column blank for now.

ABC Chart

Target Behavior:

Antecedent What happened before the behavior?	Behavior Describe the behavior	Consequence What happened after the behavior?	Function

Identifying the Function

Next, you will use the information you collected in columns A, B, and C as clues to make the best guess at which of the four functions is the reason the behavior is happening. As you can see in the below example, it can be helpful to circle the clues within the ABC notes to help guide your decision.

ABC Chart Example

Target Behavior: Elopement (leaving designated area without permission)

Antecedent What happened before the behavior?	Behavior Describe the behavior	Consequence What happened after the behavior?	Function
Teacher informed the class that there is a change in schedule today due to a morning assembly.	Student ran out of the classroom. Remained in hallway for eight minutes.	Paraprofessional talked to the student about why the assembly is important and attempted to redirect to coping skills.	Escape
Instruction to line up at end of recess.	Student ran away from the playground and toward the school exit. Remained near exit door for five minutes.	Teacher continued giving the instruction to line up.	Escape
Playing a game with a peer and lost.	Screamed at the student, threw the game pieces at them, and ran outside. Remained outside for 12 minutes.	Paraprofessional followed student as he walked around campus. Continued to provide instructions to return to class.	Escape
Teacher put on video of a book being read aloud.	Student ran to the hallway. Remained in hallway for seven minutes.	Paraprofessional attempted to redirect to coping skills. When student saw that the video had ended, he returned to class.	Escape

Function: ___Escape___

Your Turn!

Fill out the chart below for the next four times the target behavior occurs. Look for clues to what is happening before or after the behavior. Use these clues to determine the function for each time the behavior occurred, and then identify which was the most common.

Go back to your previous ABC data. Which of the four functions is being observed in each occurrence of the target behavior? Or which function is occurring the most? Some behaviors may be controlled by multiple functions, meaning the individual may be engaging in the behavior for several reasons. Look to see which occurs most often and start there!

ABC Chart

Target Behavior:

Antecedent	Behavior	Consequence	Function
What happened before the behavior?	Describe the behavior	What happened after the behavior?	

Function: _____

Let's Talk Transitions

Why are transitions so difficult? We often say that transitions are challenging for our students, but when you look closer, it's not necessarily the transition itself. And when you dive a little deeper, it is not every single transition either. So why do some transitions feel more challenging than others?

In many cases, it is when a student is going from a preferred activity to a non-preferred one, for example, going from center time to desk work or going from recess to carpet time. It's not the actual transition; it is the three demands that the transition requires, usually in a very short time when we are teaching in a typical school setting where we are following school-designated schedules.

Let's look at a common, difficult transition: going from a preferred to a non-preferred activity.

First, we are asking the students to stop doing the activity that they are enjoying. Then we ask them to clean up (i.e., give up the toys, items, and activities they are currently doing), which is hard, and then finally, we ask them to move to a less fun or preferred activity.

1. Stop doing something fun.
2. Give up toys, items, and activities they are enjoying.
3. Moving to an activity that is less fun and enjoyable.

Moreover, in the rhythm of a classroom day, there's an inherent urgency to transitions—swiftly moving from one task to the next or one location to another, whether it's cleaning up center times, lining up for recess, preparing for lunch in the cafeteria, or gathering up books to take to the library. Our aim is to make these transitions as smooth and stress-free as possible. But how do we do that when we have one or more students who struggle with these transitions?

We provide predictable routines, visual supports, transition warnings, transition cues like a bell or clean-up song, visual times, and transition objects. In the classroom, these are vital tools that boost students' ability to plan, focus, and complete tasks effectively and ease tricky transitions. These tools set students up for successful transitions and help build executive functioning skills, even at a very young age.

When thinking about the ABC data of a transition, there are two clear functions that relate: access (they want to continue with the activity, and we're denying that) and escape (they don't want to start the next task). With this new understanding, we can choose strategies that cater to these needs. Given these three challenging instructions for young learners to stop, clean up, and work, it's an ideal moment to proactively assist the student in utilizing their coping strategies and use effective behavior strategies.

Try these strategies to help with transitions

- Providing Choices
- 3 Reward Options
- Token Boards
- Range of Rewards
- Priming
- Visual Schedule
- Self-Regulation
- Firm, but Flexible
- Pause, Redirect, Reward

An Approachable Guide to FBAs

When students face challenges in school, it's crucial to understand the underlying reasons to provide effective support. These challenges, whether academic or behavioral, can stem from various factors that need to be addressed comprehensively. For instance, behaviors may result from a mismatch between the curriculum and students' current needs, as discussed later in "Accommodations vs. Modifications" on page 79. Additionally, past trauma can significantly influence present behavior, as explored in our "Embodying a Trauma-Informed Approach" section on page 60. Before proceeding to conduct a Functional Behavior Assessment (FBA), teachers should first explore classwide strategies, as highlighted in "Understanding a Tiered Approach to Student Support" on page 23, as these strategies can effectively support 85% of students. In the Tools chapter, you'll find a "Classwide Strategies Checklist" to self-assess and gather inspiration for implementing new strategies to better support struggling students in your classroom.

Classwide Strategies to Try:
- Positive Greetings at the Door
- Whole Class Reward System
- Classroom Setup
- Classwide Priming and Providing Choices
- Scheduled Breaks

It's crucial to emphasize that if a student's behavior poses a risk of harm or is unsafe, requesting an FBA to promptly develop a Behavior Intervention Plan (BIP) is the ethical course of action, with safety as the top priority. Through FBAs, behavior experts can pinpoint the environmental triggers, unmet needs, or areas for needed skill development that may be contributing to the challenging behaviors. From this, they can create a targeted Behavior Intervention Plan (BIP), which is a carefully curated package of behavior strategies aimed at supporting a particular student in both reducing challenging behaviors and building essential skills. In this section, we'll outline the steps to completing an FBA and provide practical tips to ensure this assessment is both easy and effective.

Step 1. Familiarize

- Read past records and background information
- Familiarize yourself with what is already in place
- Send requests to set up family and teacher interviews

3 Questions To Ask Yourself:
- Is there a history of trauma?
- What are the long-term goals for this student?
- If there are behavior goals in place, what is the current data?

Step 2. Prepare

- Connect with the family and teacher to explain your role
- Send a thorough interview form to learn as much as you can prior to the observation (Our interview form is included in *"An Approachable Guide to FBAs"* pdf, available at ABAVisualized.com)
- Schedule observations on different days, during different activities

Step 3. Observe

- Note accommodations and modifications observed
- Describe classwide strategies being used (See "Classwide Strategies Checklist" in our Tools chapter)
- Record patterns of any challenging behaviors as well as moments of success

Step 4. Collaborate

- Interview families about their main concerns and goals
- Interview teacher to learn what is working and what they need more support with
- Connect with other service providers to ensure overall goals are aligned

3 Collaborative Questions to Ask:
- What do you already have in place that's working well?
- What activity or situation would you like the most support with?
- What ideas do you have for how we could better support this student?

Step 5. Analyze

- Review your data to identify target behavior, its function, and baseline rates
- Identify an appropriate replacement behavior
- Look for specific triggers and moments of success to help inspire your upcoming recommendations

How Do I Choose A Replacement Behavior?

Ask yourself, "Does the student have an effective way to consistently communicate their needs?" If not, start here. Research has demonstrated that functional communication training (FCT) effectively reduces 90% of challenging behaviors.

Replacement behaviors that teach functional communication:
- Asking for break (from work)
- Asking for break (to engage in sensory activities)
- Asking for help
- Asking for space
- Asking for items/activities
- Asking for more information
- Asking for more time
- Asking for a delay in starting a task

If the student is consistently and effectively communicating, ask yourself, "Does the student demonstrate independent self-regulation of a variety of coping skills?" If not, then build on functional communication by teaching coping strategies.

Replacement behaviors that teach self-regulation:
- Engaging in breathing exercises
- Using stress balls, weighted blankets, or other sensory items
- Engaging in movement activity for sensory input
- Requesting to use the Calm Corner
- Engaging in mindfulness activities
- Using positive self-talk

If the student is effectively communicating and using self-regulation strategies, ask yourself, "Does the student demonstrate age–appropriate executive-functioning skills?" If not, then aim to build a variety of executive-functioning skills that can help support building better behaviors, while still honoring any uses of functional communication or emotional-regulation strategies.

<u>Replacement behaviors that teach executive-functioning skills:</u>
- Initiating tasks
- Sustained attention
- Flexibility
- Frustration tolerance
- Inhibitory control

Step 6. Plan

- Adopt a mindset of adding to what's already working, rather than starting fresh
- Prioritize establishing clear expectations and clear, motivating rewards
- Propose two to three strategy options to the team and ask which they prefer (Learn more about collaborative decision-making in our recorded course, Coaching with Impact, available at ABAVisualized.com)

<u>Six Questions to Ask Yourself to Determine if a BIP is Needed:</u>
1. Is the behavior potentially dangerous to self or others?
2. Does the behavior impede learning for self or others?
3. Does the behavior impede the student's ability to form meaningful peer relationships?
4. Have medical needs been addressed?
5. Have academic needs been addressed? (e.g. accommodations and modifications)
6. Have schoolwide & classwide strategies already been put in place?

Step 7. Recommend

Did you know the typical amount of time that behavior recommendations are implemented correctly is only 7-10 days?! Let's fix this!
- Propose least restrictive ideas first, such as classwide strategies and accommodations
- Consider what is actually feasible in that setting
- Write your BIP in approachable language for easier follow-through for the whole team! (Use BIP Visualized to build your own step-by-step visual behavior plans that boost buy-in, accuracy, and ease! Available at bipvisualized.com)

Making Behavior Recommendations in IEPs

In this section, we will explore the purpose and process of behavior recommendations in Individualized Education Programs (IEPs). The purpose of behavior recommendations in an IEP is to address any behaviors that may impede a student's ability to access their education. These behaviors can range from minor disruptions to more severe challenges that significantly impact the student's academic performance or social interactions. By identifying these behaviors and creating targeted recommendations, we can ensure that each student receives the support they need and hold the team accountable for implementing them. When deciding what behavior recommendations to include in your student's IEP, consider the three following questions.

1. Do they need accommodations/modifications to support better behaviors?

Before considering a Behavior Intervention Plan (BIP), we need to ensure that students have access to a curriculum tailored to their level, along with necessary accommodations and modifications determined by the IEP team. For instance, if a 5th-grade student is reading at a 2nd-grade level, they might engage in "task refusal" or even high-intensity challenging behaviors when assigned 5th-grade level reading tasks. In these situations, behavior strategies might not work effectively because the behaviors stem from a mismatch between the student's reading level and the difficulty of the assigned tasks, rather than the student's motivation. It's crucial to avoid unfair expectations. During behavior observations conducted for a Functional Behavior Assessment (FBA), it's beneficial to use the student's

Example Accommodations

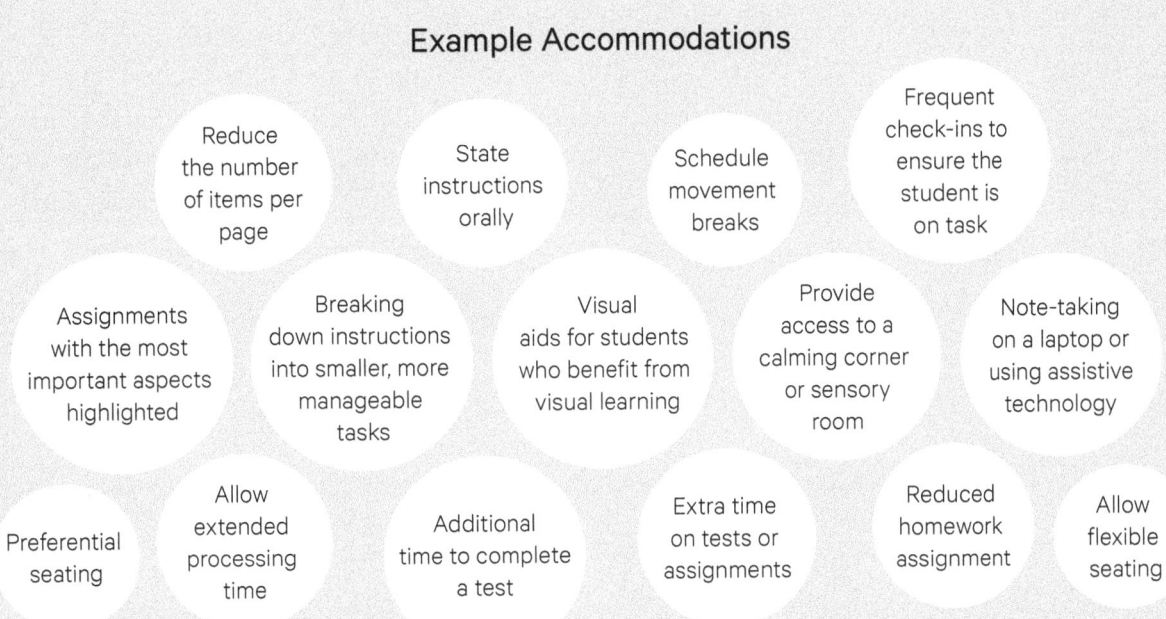

Reduce the number of items per page

State instructions orally

Schedule movement breaks

Frequent check-ins to ensure the student is on task

Assignments with the most important aspects highlighted

Breaking down instructions into smaller, more manageable tasks

Visual aids for students who benefit from visual learning

Provide access to a calming corner or sensory room

Note-taking on a laptop or using assistive technology

Preferential seating

Allow extended processing time

Additional time to complete a test

Extra time on tests or assignments

Reduced homework assignment

Allow flexible seating

accommodations and modifications as a checklist. This helps to determine which supports are currently being utilized, which ones are effective, and whether any adjustments are necessary.

Understanding the difference between accommodations and modifications is essential. It allows us to support each student's unique learning path effectively. As teachers, our role in applying and adapting these strategies is vital for creating an inclusive and supportive learning environment. When we use accommodations, we alter HOW a student learns. When we use modifications, we adjust WHAT a student is taught. Accommodations help students access the same curriculum as their peers, while modifications change the curriculum to a lower or higher level. As students transition into middle school and high school, modifications can influence their academic paths, potentially altering their trajectory toward either a diploma track or a certificate track.

"I thrived best when teachers offered adaptations within assignments/homework where I could demonstrate that I understood the concepts and topic, but could demonstrate it in my own way."

Denis Yunis

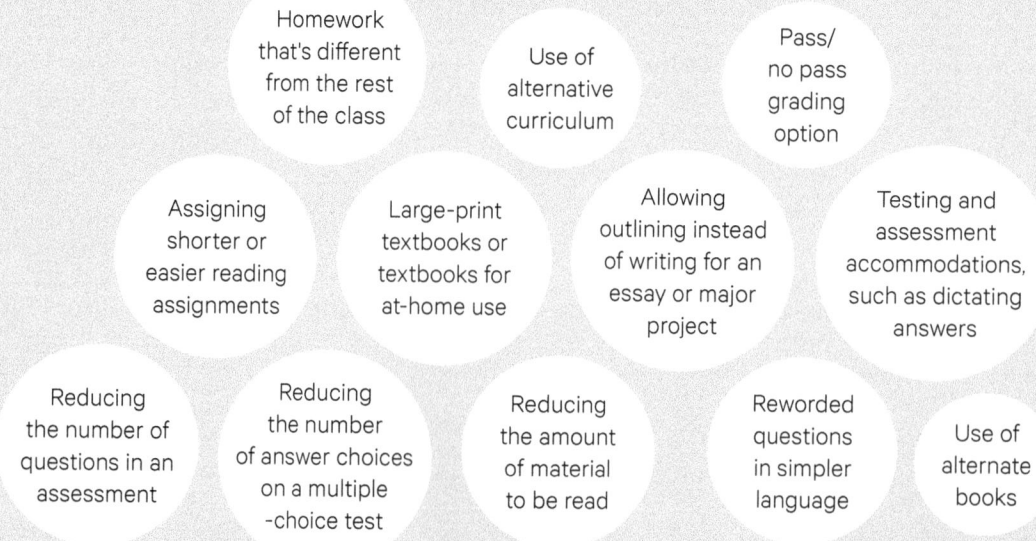

Example Modifications

- Homework that's different from the rest of the class
- Use of alternative curriculum
- Pass/ no pass grading option
- Assigning shorter or easier reading assignments
- Large-print textbooks or textbooks for at-home use
- Allowing outlining instead of writing for an essay or major project
- Testing and assessment accommodations, such as dictating answers
- Reducing the number of questions in an assessment
- Reducing the number of answer choices on a multiple -choice test
- Reducing the amount of material to be read
- Reworded questions in simpler language
- Use of alternate books

2. Have we considered the least-restrictive environment (LRE)?

LRE is not a location; it is a level of support. It is always an IEP team decision!

Choosing a classroom placement is a crucial part of an individualized support plan for students with academic or developmental diagnoses. While these options vary greatly from school district to school district, many schools offer general education classrooms and special education classrooms (although the wording may differ). General education classrooms are comprised of a majority of students without special education eligibility and follow the grade level curriculum developed by the state or national standards. A special education classroom is a setting that supports students with disabilities. They often have a higher staff-to-student ratio and modified curriculums, allowing for a more individualized approach to supporting students. In this setting, classwork is often broken down into smaller steps, visual supports are more regularly used, paraprofessionals and staff will usually have more behavioral training, and there are more opportunities for collaboration with service providers.

Students typically have more access to individualized rewards and breaks, and teachers incorporate building communication and daily living skills throughout the day. A special education setting may benefit students who struggle with following high-paced whole-group instructions, have yet to establish sustained attending skills, have difficulty following directions the first time asked, or when the academic level is too challenging. Often, these classrooms are comprised of students who could benefit from more support with behavioral needs, academics, social skills, and daily living skills. While these neurodiverse students are in their special education classroom for most academic activities, there are still opportunities for them to participate in the general education setting, including joining in specials (e.g. Art, Music, PE), lunch, recess, assemblies, and field trips.

With increasing awareness of the positive impacts of early diagnosis and early intervention, classrooms are becoming more and more neurodiverse. An inclusive classroom is a general education classroom where students with and without academic and developmental differences learn together. There are many benefits of inclusion for both the students with disabilities and their neurotypical peers. Some of these include more opportunities to naturally learn from peers, creating a more-accepting class culture, furthering academic learning, improving later access to employment, and fostering an understanding that differences don't mean "less than."

In 2021, researchers Roldan, Marauri, Aubert, and Flecha interviewed teachers, students, and school volunteers about their learning environments. One neurotypical student, Ana, who was a classmate of another student with Autism, José, explained that getting to know him in the school allowed her to learn about diversity in a way that she could not have done before, even saying getting to know José "turned her life around."

> "José has taught me that many times people have barriers because we all have barriers, whether at the time of learning, at the time of adults finding a job... there is always a way to overcome them, and José has taught me many things. In fact, I think he has taught me more than I have taught him."

Ana's experience exemplifies how inclusion can benefit many students, not just those with disabilities. Teachers also positively described their experiences with inclusion settings as

> "interactive learning environments where students learn from others, generating opportunities to acknowledge and normalize human diversity."

One teacher said, "They are all integrated. They always look the same to each other; they do know that one has more difficulties in one thing or another, but they all treat each other equally." Teachers shared that their inclusive classrooms led to a culture of acceptance and respect toward others. They described that students began to understand that "children could learn at different paces and that they can need different kinds of support or adapted materials, but this does not mean that they cannot share the experience of learning."

Understanding the continuum of LRE is essential for fostering inclusive educational settings where every student can succeed. It's important to normalize the understanding that students may require diverse levels of support, services, and classroom placements, and that this variability is entirely acceptable. While the specifics of the continuum may vary across school districts or even among different campuses within the same district, the underlying principle remains consistent: to provide each student with the appropriate level of support necessary for their academic, behavioral, and social development. Below, we outline the general flow of the continuum from the least to the most restrictive settings.

LRE Continuum

Least
Restrictive

General education without support

General education with support
(Full inclusion)

General education with pull-out services
(e.g. Speech, OT, PT, Counseling, Adapted PE, social skills, etc.)

Itinerant teacher
(Push-in or meet with general ed. teacher for consult)

Inclusion classroom
(General ed. with special ed. teacher support or co-teaching)

Resource room pull-out services for academics
(e.g. Reading, writing, math)

Self-contained classroom
(Mild/moderate or moderate/severe)

Alternative educational placement

Most
Restrictive

Homebound or home hospital instruction
(e.g. Nonpublic school, facility, or residential program)

3. Do they require behavior service minutes to target skill-building goals, or can these skills be taught through regular instruction or existing services?

Once the team has determined which skill-building goals will replace challenging behaviors, it's important to consider how and when these skills will be taught proactively. At times, teachers can incorporate skill-building into the regular classroom schedule. Alternatively, for students already attending counseling, speech therapy, or occupational therapy sessions, behavior replacement skills might also be taught during these sessions. For example, counseling sessions can focus on self-regulation, Speech-Language Pathologists can teach functional communication skills, and Occupational Therapists can teach sensory-regulation strategies.

For students requiring more individualized behavior support, dedicated behavior service minutes may be needed. These services would target proactive teaching of the replacement skills, individualized feedback and encouragement, and the implementation of the Behavior Intervention Plan (BIP) strategies throughout the day. The team may also determine that the student would benefit from a one-on-one aide to support with behavior and/or academics. These decisions should be collectively made during the IEP meeting, ensuring a well-defined plan detailing how, when, and by whom the skill-building goals will be taught.

If it is found that a BIP is necessary in addition to the existing supports, refer to the next section for further guidance!

Rethinking Behavior Intervention Plans

When a student is engaging in behaviors that have the potential to cause harm or impede learning, it is beneficial to conduct a Functional Behavior Assessment (FBA) to identify the underlying reasons behind the behavior and develop individualized recommendations. Based on this assessment, an individualized support plan, known as a Behavior Intervention Plan (BIP), is created. A BIP is a carefully curated selection of behavior strategies that aim to reduce challenging behavior and teach replacement skills. Despite the considerable research supporting the positive impact of BIPs, there are many common barriers that often impede their potential effectiveness.

Barriers Impacting Effective BIPs

Effective Training

In our survey of over 200 individuals responsible for developing BIPs, only 43% reported feeling confident choosing strategies to fit individual student needs. In this same survey, 79.4% reported initially not feeling prepared to independently develop a BIP and only 35% of respondents reported currently feeling effective at disseminating their plan to their staff and stakeholders.

When we asked these experts to complete this sentence, "When I first was expected to write behavior plans independently, I felt...", the answers were alarming: "like I was thrown in;" "completely overwhelmed;" "like I had to learn through trial and error;" "terrified;" "unsure;" "stressed;" "lost;" "nervous;" and "I felt so much pressure."

Technical Jargon

The complexity and confusion associated with commonly used, technical behavior terminology contributes to the abandonment of potentially beneficial BIPs. This abandonment leaves teachers feeling under-supported and behavior experts feeling ineffective.

Technical language negatively affects comprehension and acceptability of evidence-based strategies, particularly for individuals with little or no training in Applied Behavior Analysis (ABA) principles. In our own survey of over 500 respondents, we found that 90% of teachers and parents expressed a greater likelihood of using behavior strategies if they were presented in a more understandable manner. This difficulty in understanding likely contributes to research findings indicating that team members implement fewer than 60% of the strategies outlined in a BIP, with an average accuracy rate of only 68% when implemented.

Time

In our pilot study, we discovered that the average time spent developing a BIP was 3.6 hours. While Board Certified Behavior Analysts (BCBAs) have genuine intentions to develop an individualized support plan that considers the student's preferences, strengths, and needs, as well as the practicalities for the team, the demanding nature of this process consumes a considerable amount of time and effort.

In fact, "time" was the number one barrier reported by behavior experts in our pilot study interviews. Many behavior experts and teachers face constraints on their time, limiting their ability to dedicate the necessary resources for creating comprehensive and tailored BIPs. This time limitation may compromise the thoroughness and quality of BIPs, impacting their overall effectiveness in supporting students with diverse needs.

Traditional Teaching Methods

After a behavior expert has developed a BIP, the traditional method of teaching this plan to the team involves providing them with a multi-page text document and reviewing it together. However, our surveys and research indicate that this method is not effective for optimal learning and retention, and it does not adequately support those who could benefit from the plan.

In our pilot study, the average number of strategies included in a BIP was 26 (ranging from 4 to 45), while those responsible for implementation were only able to recall an average of 3 strategies (ranging from 0 to 5). This discrepancy aligns with established research on memory retention, which indicates that information presented in dense text is prone to being forgotten. The brain quickly loses information, tends to overlook the middle portions of lengthy texts, and may become overwhelmed by dense material.

The Power of *Visuals*

Visuals have long been known to amplify understanding, retention, and engagement when learning new skills. Within the fields of Applied Behavior Analysis (ABA) and Special Education, the positive influence of using visuals to support learners is widely accepted and celebrated. Visual supports have become indispensable tools in homes and classrooms. Yet, there's a noticeable gap in leveraging visual teaching when it comes to supporting parents, educators, and behavior support staff.

ABA Visualized is proud to be the first to take an innovative approach to teaching evidence-based behavior strategies through step-by-step visuals, making complex information more approachable, accessible, and relatable. Inspired by the many stories shared about the positive impact of visuals in behavior support, we are taking this work one step further by creating an online platform that makes behavior expertise accessible through visuals. BIP Visualized allows behavior professionals to create and customize their own visual behavior plans, access a growing library of visual strategies, resources, and on-demand trainings developed in collaboration with autistic consultants, and share everything directly with families, teachers, and behavior staff. This is the only platform built to support behavior planning, learning, and collaboration entirely through visuals.

With any of our new products, first comes a research deep dive to fully understand current barriers and experiences. In the following infographic, we're highlighting research findings comparing text-based learning with visual learning. We explore established multidisciplinary research on the efficacy of visuals versus text and reveal insights specific to the field of ABA. We've also been busy collecting our own research! With the recognized success of ABA Visualized's signature visual teaching style, we have been testing the impact of applying this approach to developing and disseminating Behavior Intervention Plans (BIPs). We're finding that teaching families and educators through text leads to low buy-in, low engagement, low understanding, and most importantly, low impact on the learner. Further, in our survey of over 200 behavior experts, only 35% reported feeling effective with their current teaching approach. Instead, when behavior strategies are taught through visuals, families and educators are more engaged, have better understanding, remember the skills longer, implement it more accurately, and feel more confident!

We're excited to share some of these findings with you, some of which may be eye-opening when considering their implications for the quality of services and care provided to our learners and their stakeholders. Our hope is that by highlighting the power of visuals, you will feel inspired to become a visual storyteller yourself!

Teaching with Text
The Traditional Way

Low Understanding

Text often leads to low understanding, which hinders parents' ability to advocate for their child's needs and potentially causes misinterpretation of recommended strategies.

(Banks et al., 2018; Critchfield et al., 2017)

Low Acceptance

The use of technical language in behavior recommendations can lead to reduced acceptance of the recommendations, particularly among individuals with little or no training in ABA principles. In fact, researchers found that people rate ABA jargon as "not motivating" and "unpleasant."

(Banks et al., 2018; Critchfield et al., 2017)

Low Engagement

Teaching through complex text can lead to low engagement because the team may struggle to follow behavior recommendations and resist change when the language is overly technical or hard to understand.

(Banks et al., 2018; Critchfield et al., 2017)

Low Accessibility

Text is not always accessible to everyone, as language barriers, especially for families with limited English proficiency, can hinder understanding and communication during behavior intervention discussions, leading to reduced parental engagement, misunderstandings, and increased stress and anxiety related to their child's needs.

(Andrade, Hancock, & Whaley, 2019; Bradshaw & Richey, 2015; Hatcher et al., 2016, Taylor & Landrum, 2016)

Low Confidence

Complex technical behavior recommendations can lead to low confidence as they often result in confusion, stress, and ineffective implementation, leaving stakeholders feeling unsupported and service providers ineffective.

In our own survey of people responsible for implementing behavior strategies, only 40% reported feeling confident and only 28% reported feeling prepared.

Feeling confident in using strategies

40%

Feeling prepared to support behaviors

28%

(Banks et al., 2018; Holt et al., 2016; Jarmolowicz et al., 2008; McMahon, Feldberg, & Ardoin, 2021)

Low Accuracy

Research shows that typical teaching approaches result in low accuracy with team members implementing less than 60% of the recommended strategies, and those being done so with an average accuracy rate of only 68%.

Parents and teachers report struggling to understand and implement complex technical instructions effectively.

Strategies implemented

60%

Accuracy of implemented strategies

68%

(de Bruin et al., 2014; Scheibel et al., 2022; Walker et al., 2021)

Low Collaboration

The use of technical language in behavior strategies often creates communication barriers, hindering effective collaboration between behavior specialists and stakeholders like parents and teachers.

In our own survey, only 25% of people responsible for implementing behavior strategies reported being aware of what strategies were being used in other settings.

(Peterson et al., 2018; Sailor & McCarthy, 2015)

Difficult to Remember

Text is easy to forget because our brain quickly loses information, we often overlook the middle parts of long texts, and dense material can overwhelm us.

In our pilot study, we found the average number of strategies included in a BIP was 26. However, the average number of strategies a person responsible for implementing could recall was only 3.

(The Forgetting Curve, Serial Position Effect, Cognitive Load Theory)

The Forgetting Curve for Text

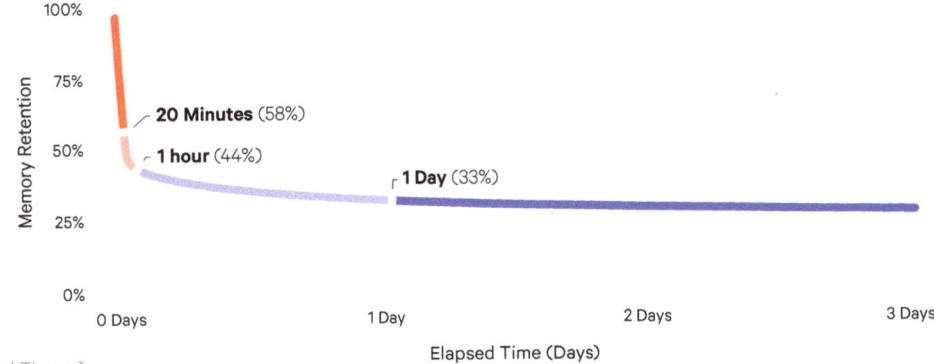

20 Minutes (58%)
1 hour (44%)
1 Day (33%)

Memory Retention — 100%, 75%, 50%, 25%, 0%

Elapsed Time (Days) — 0 Days, 1 Day, 2 Days, 3 Days

Teaching with Images
Our Innovative Approach

Better Understanding

Visuals make things easier to understand and they help teachers and parents better grasp behavior management strategies, making learning and skill application more effective.

(Albers & Greer, 2010; Eberhard, K., 2021; Hughes & Frederick, 2006; Sung-Hee, K., 2022)

More Preferred

Research has shown that most people overwhelmingly prefer instructions with visuals and find them easier to use than traditional written instructions, indicating a clear preference for visuals over text-based content.

(Graff & Karsten, 2012)

More Engagement

Visuals improve engagement by capturing and holding the viewer's attention more effectively, as shown through eye-tracking studies. Visual storytelling makes the content more memorable, and viewers engage longer.

(Harsh et al., 2019; HubSpot, 2022; Paradi, D., 1986)

More Accessible for Diverse Needs

Visuals offer greater accessibility, ensuring that those with diverse needs can access and understand the information.

(Abdulrahaman, et al., 2020)

Increased Confidence

Training with visual supports has been shown to boost confidence among parents and teachers in managing challenging behaviors.

(Clees & Brady, 2006)

Better Collaboration

The use of visuals has been shown to enhance communication between service providers, parents and teachers, fostering more effective collaboration in behavior management.

(Zarcone & Lindauer, 2006)

Higher Accuracy

Visuals significantly improve accuracy in comprehension, recall, and implementation, as seen in studies where infographics led to better understanding, and instructions with diagrams resulted in a substantial increase in accuracy from 38% to 99%.

Remembering textual content

 38%

Remembering visual content

 99%

Additionally, visual supports have been shown to enhance the fidelity of implementing behavior strategies in both special education and general classroom settings.

(Arco & Ricci, 2018; Graff & Karsten, 2012; Koegel & Koegel, 2006; Meyer & Bohning, 2011)

Better Retention

Using visuals alongside words makes information easier to remember because it engages different parts of the brain, reduces mental effort, and helps people see and remember relationships and patterns, ultimately improving retention.

Research has shown that people tend to remember information with visuals significantly better than text alone (65% compared to 10%), which is widely understood as "the pictorial superiority effect."

Remembering textual content

 10%

Remembering visual content

 65%

In our own pilot study, accurate recall improved by 57% when behavior strategies were presented as visuals instead of text.

(Dual Coding Theory, The Picture Superiority Effect, Cognitive Load Theory)

BIP Visualized

BIP Visualized is an online platform that makes behavior expertise more accessible through visuals. It supports behavior professionals in creating and customizing visual Behavior Intervention Plans while also providing a growing library of visual strategies, resources, and on demand trainings developed in collaboration with autistic consultants. All materials are designed to be shared directly with families, educators, and behavior staff.

While BIPs are well supported by research, many providers report challenges when plans are long, technical, or difficult for teams to understand and implement consistently. BIP Visualized replaces traditional text heavy approaches with step by step visual tools that are easier to learn, teach, and apply across settings. This visual approach supports clearer communication, stronger follow through, and more consistent support for learners at home, in schools, and in the community.

Try it out at **BIPVisualized.com**

"As a seasoned BCBA, I can confidently say that BIP Visualized is a game-changer for the field of Applied Behavior Analysis"

Steven Camp, CEO at CAMP

"Please make this part of your toolbox of resources, you will not be disappointed!"

Shayla, School Psychologist at Fresno USD

"BIP Visualized is AMAZING!!! It's a lifesaver for BCBAs, a visual map for families, and filled with strategies everyone can use immediately."

Julia Bernasconi, BCBA

How a Visual Behavior Plan Works

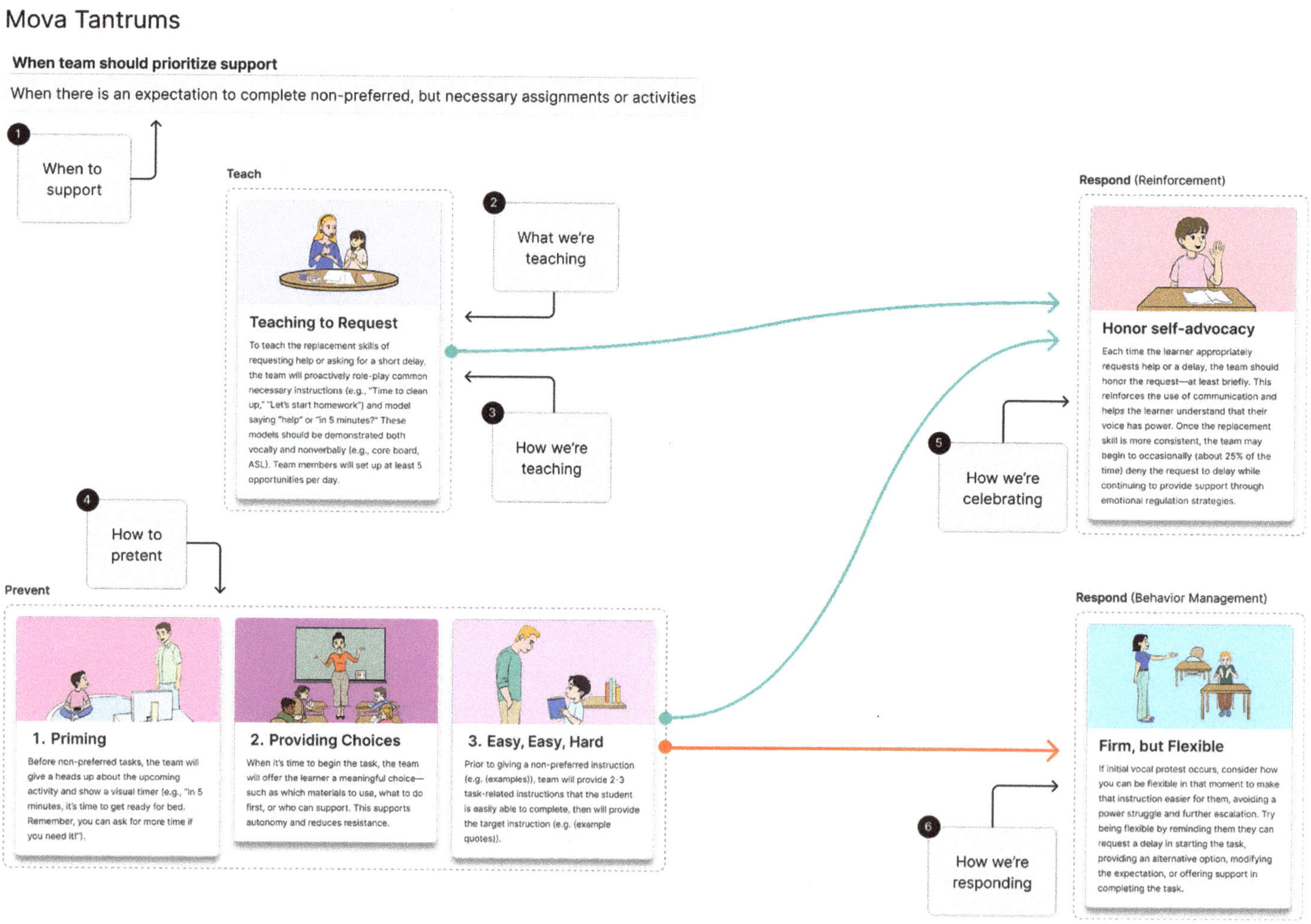

Mova Tantrums

When team should prioritize support

When there is an expectation to complete non-preferred, but necessary assignments or activities

1 When to support

Teach

Teaching to Request

To teach the replacement skills of requesting help or asking for a short delay, the team will proactively role-play common necessary instructions (e.g., "Time to clean up," "Let's start homework") and model saying "help" or "in 5 minutes?" These models should be demonstrated both vocally and nonverbally (e.g., core board, ASL). Team members will set up at least 5 opportunities per day.

2 What we're teaching

3 How we're teaching

4 How to pretent

Prevent

1. Priming

Before non-preferred tasks, the team will give a heads up about the upcoming activity and show a visual timer (e.g., "In 5 minutes, it's time to get ready for bed. Remember, you can ask for more time if you need it!").

2. Providing Choices

When it's time to begin the task, the team will offer the learner a meaningful choice— such as which materials to use, what to do first, or who can support. This supports autonomy and reduces resistance.

3. Easy, Easy, Hard

Prior to giving a non-preferred instruction (e.g. (examples)), team will provide 2-3 task-related instructions that the student is easily able to complete, then will provide the target instruction (e.g. (example quotes)).

Respond (Reinforcement)

Honor self-advocacy

Each time the learner appropriately requests help or a delay, the team should honor the request—at least briefly. This reinforces the use of communication and helps the learner understand that their voice has power. Once the replacement skill is more consistent, the team may begin to occasionally (about 25% of the time) deny the request to delay while continuing to provide support through emotional regulation strategies.

5 How we're celebrating

Respond (Behavior Management)

Firm, but Flexible

If initial vocal protest occurs, consider how you can be flexible in that moment to make that instruction easier for them, avoiding a power struggle and further escalation. Try being flexible by reminding them they can request a delay in starting the task, providing an alternative option, modifying the expectation, or offering support in completing the task.

6 How we're responding

What Makes Us Different

Save time without sacrificing quality

Clear step-by-step visuals

Focus on practical real-life applications

Neurodiversity-affirming

Unlimited sharing

Trainings for the whole team

What You Can Do with BIP Visualized

Create Your Own Visual BIP

Go to "Create a visual BIP" and simply drag and drop evidence-based strategies to build a visual step-by-step plan for your team!

Features
~ Easy fill-in-the-blank descriptions
~ Fully customizable strategies
~ Print, download, or share
~ Real-time co-editing

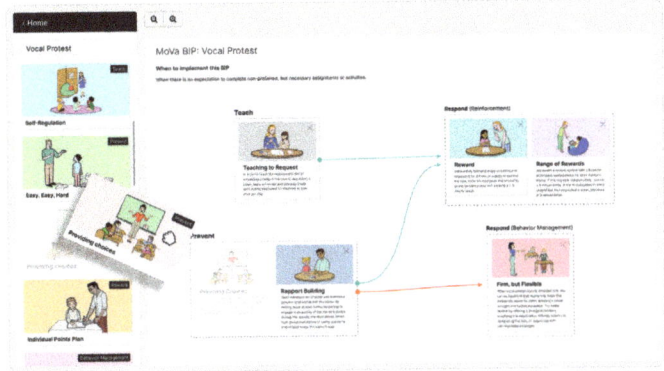

Edit and Customize Strategies

Edit strategies with your own images and text to make them completely individualized. Just click "Edit" on the top right of any strategy to customize!

Features
~ Upload images
~ Edit text
~ Save as template to reuse

Explore Courses and Resources to Share

Access a growing collection of trainings and resources to expand your own clinical expertise & support your team between sessions! Your account includes unlimited sharing, so your team can access everything you share— completely free.

We have trainings for
~ CEU trainings for BCBAs
~ Shareable trainings for educators
~ Shareable training for families

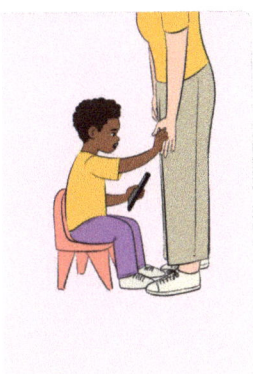

An Approachable Guide to

Smoother Transitions

A Visual Lesson for Parent Support

Created by
Morgan van Diepen, M.Ed., BCBA
Co-founder, BIP Visualized

FOR FAMILIES

Building Motivation

Introduction

Motivation comes from both intrinsic and extrinsic factors. Intrinsic motivation comes from within, while extrinsic motivation comes from external factors. When we are intrinsically motivated, we engage in an activity because we enjoy it or we feel proud of what we've accomplished. When we are extrinsically motivated, we do something in order to gain an external reward, for example, a paycheck. As adults, we thrive off of both these types of motivators.

As teachers, we recognize the significance of motivating our students. While some students may naturally possess intrinsic motivation to excel in academics and follow instructions, others may benefit from extra encouragement. Acknowledging our students' efforts, academic achievements, or positive behaviors can be as simple as adding a sticker to their paper, offering a high-five or a thumbs-up, or praising them verbally. Think about the uplifting feeling you get when your boss, colleague, friend, or partner acknowledges something you've done. It's gratifying to be appreciated! Ideally, all students, regardless of age, would be internally driven to thrive in school and consistently give their best effort. However, this isn't always feasible, just as we wouldn't work without compensation solely out of pride in our work. This concept applies to our students as well. This is why it's crucial to identify external motivators that resonate with each student individually.

This is where implementing classwide strategies like a Whole Class Reward System or individual strategies like First, Then, Token Boards, or Individual Points Plan effectively establish clear expectations and rewards. This approach can provide students with an added boost of motivation to overcome challenges, knowing they will be able to enjoy their favorite activity afterward. We can apply this strategy ourselves to build motivation for completing tasks like finishing our progress reports or affirming and attesting to an IEP. It's rewarding to celebrate our accomplishments afterward! Similarly, acknowledging students' efforts with small celebrations can significantly enhance and maintain their motivation to participate and be engaged in tasks that are difficult or non-preferred.

When we have external motivators like screen time or playing with a favorite toy, we can build and nurture our students' internal drive. Understanding what holds significance for each student is key—be it excelling academically, being a supportive friend, or making their family proud. Shifting our language from "I'm so proud of you" to "You must be so proud of yourself!" and from "I love that you're working independently" to "Look at what you achieved all on your own!" helps link their actions to intrinsic motivation. By identifying what resonates with each student personally, we foster their sense of accomplishment and pride beyond any external rewards.

Sometimes, sparking motivation requires a bit of creativity! Not every student will be inspired by the same rewards—what excites one student might not interest another. Take a look at our "Tips for Building Meaningful Rewards." Here, you'll find recommendations for individualizing your approach to recognizing and rewarding student progress.

Tips for Building Meaningful Rewards

In our classrooms, we get to make education inclusive and supportive by recognizing every effort, celebrating each milestone, and incorporating encouragement into our teaching to enhance our students' learning experience. Establishing rewards and motivation is important for all students, regardless of age. While what motivates us is different for everyone, it's an essential part of building confidence and motivation while learning new skills. Remember that involving students in this process empowers their voice and choice! Here are six tips for creating meaningful rewards that can help students stay motivated and engaged.

1. Rewards should be motivating

Creating motivation to learn is the key to success. What we find motivating or rewarding is different for everyone, and this can change daily! Before starting to teach a student any new skills, first identify what they may be motivated to earn as rewards for making progress toward their goals. You may be able to simply ask some students, but for others, you may need to pay attention to what they like by seeing how they choose to spend their free time.

Before starting to teach any new skills, identify what could potentially be motivating for the student to earn. Watch which items or activities naturally draw the student's attention. Think beyond toys and electronics. Some students may love earning special activities with a teacher or peer or getting a positive note sent home. Also, consider your students' special interests! Getting to spend time researching topics they love could be very motivating.

2. Recognition should be immediate

When learning a new skill, receiving immediate feedback is essential. As a teacher balancing the support of a classroom full of students, it can be difficult to consistently provide that in-the-moment response. This is a great opportunity for paraprofessionals to support! Identify the one or two top-priority skills you're building for each student, and work together to recognize and celebrate when the student does that skill independently.

When teaching a new skill and the student does it independently, recognize and celebrate it right away. This can look like giving behavior-specific praise, where you say exactly what they did well (e.g. "I love how you're sharing with your friend!") or giving a pre-determined reward (e.g. a star on their token board, a point for their team in a whole class reward system, etc.).

3. Reward should match effort

Consider the difficulty of the task for that student when deciding how big the reward and our excitement should be. The size of the reward should match the size of their effort. For example, if you have to provide a lot of assistance while your student is putting on their shoes, you may give a little praise at the end (e.g. "nice job pulling tight"); however, if they tie their shoes on their own, you will want to give a lot of praise and possibly an extra reward (like more time playing outside) to celebrate. Save the big rewards and big excitements for the harder skills that your student is working to learn!

The more effort the student puts in, the bigger the reward and excitement! Here, the student is completing the worksheet, but she's not really focused on the work, and you've seen better quality work from her before. We can recognize that she's on task, but we'll save the bigger rewards for when she puts in more effort. See "Range of Rewards" visual strategy, pg. 118.

4. Provide choices of rewards

Before starting an academic activity, try offering choices of rewards that students can have when they finish. For many students, it's beneficial to physically show two or three choices of activities/items that can be earned. This can also be done with a visual choice board! When the students finish the academic task, they earn their chosen reward.

Establishing rewards ahead of time can build motivation for both individual students and the whole class. Providing a variety of choices for these rewards allows students to have more autonomy, fostering responsibility and intrinsic motivation.

5. Make rewards special

To maximize motivation, rewards should be special and tailored to students' interests. Consider creating a treasure box filled with items or activities that students help pick out, or have them vote for classwide rewards or parties to earn. Incorporating surprise rewards can also add excitement and anticipation. Remember to keep the rewards reserved for teaching moments, rotating items to maintain interest and motivation over time.

Ensure that rewards remain a special incentive by involving students in the selection process and making it a collaborative decision. Encourage them to suggest items or activities they find motivating and enjoyable. By keeping the rewards fresh and engaging, students will feel a sense of ownership and excitement in working toward achieving their goals.

6. Build intrinsic motivation

To foster intrinsic motivation in skill learning, celebrate every step of progress while gradually shifting focus from external rewards to internal satisfaction. Acknowledge their achievements with statements like, "You did that on your own! I bet you feel so proud!" or "You took care of yourself when you felt angry; you should be proud of yourself!" Emphasize celebrating independence and effort, even amidst mistakes, to instill a sense of pride and accomplishment in students.

For new skills: celebrate every attempt and every step in progressing toward independence. Once they have learned to do the skill on their own, fade out the amount of praise and reinforcement you are giving. To help encourage that intrinsic motivation and pride, start shifting your language from phrases like, "I love that you're sharing!" to "You're being such a good friend!"

Choosing a motivation strategy

Choosing a motivation strategy is inherently individualized, just like every aspect of supporting students. Each student possesses unique interests, strengths, and challenges that influence what drives them. What sparks enthusiasm in one student may not have the same effect on another. Therefore, teachers must tailor their approach to motivation based on a thorough understanding of each student's preferences and needs. By recognizing and honoring these individual differences, educators can cultivate an environment where every student feels valued and empowered to reach their full potential. Just as we personalize instruction and accommodations, so too must we personalize our motivation strategies to ensure every student is engaged and motivated to succeed. For teachers seeking to create more motivation among all students, starting with Providing Choices and implementing the Whole Class Reward System can be effective strategies. For those looking for support in developing a Behavior Intervention Plan (BIP), we recommend reviewing the 3 Reward Options visual strategy. For younger students, especially those in pre-K or transition programs, it's recommended to begin with approaches like First, Then, Providing Choices, and/or Token Boards. It's important to note that while most students will benefit from classwide strategies, approximately 5% may require individualized support. Understanding this tiered approach to student support is essential for effectively meeting the diverse needs of all learners (See pg. 23 for more on this).

3 Ways to a Set-up Whole Class Reward System

Met criteria ✔ Gets reward

Independent
"to each their own"

Example
Anyone who earns 10 points gets a reward

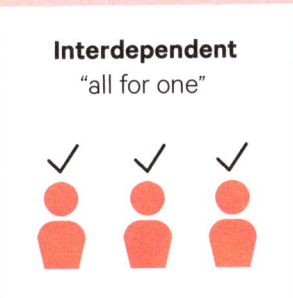

Interdependent
"all for one"

Example
The whole team has to earn 10 points for the whole team to get a reward

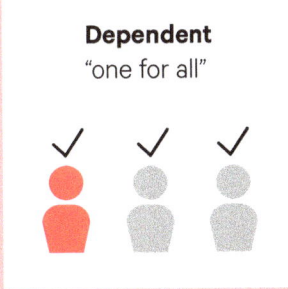

Dependent
"one for all"

Example
If one person on the team earns 10 points, the whole team gets a reward

Whole Class Reward System

A whole class reward system is a classroom management method where the entire class collaborates to earn rewards by meeting predetermined goals or behavioral expectations set by the teacher. It's a structured, positive approach where teachers create the "rules" or expectations for the rewards. When you first start using this system with students, it's best to set your points goal to be small! You want as many students as possible to earn the reward the first few days of this system so that they can fully understand the rules and expectations that you have set and feel that this goal is attainable, creating more motivation. Over time, you can create larger and larger point goals and adjust student expectations throughout the school year. An example of this class reward system could be a teacher putting a pom-pom in a jar sitting on her desk when students are working quietly. Maybe after the jar is filled, they will earn an extra recess or a special treat. Below are the three types of whole-class rewards (or types of "group contingencies"). The overall structure of a whole class reward system remains the same across these three variations by establishing class-wide expectations, choosing motivating rewards, and letting students achieve these rewards by fulfilling the expectations. It's up to you which you choose, but to help you pick, we've outlined some pros and cons and described each variation.

To Each Their Own (independent group contingency)

No teams are established. Set a goal for the number of points needed to earn during your chosen activity in order to earn the reward. Any student who meets the goal earns the reward. Pros: a fair approach where each student has control over whether they earn the reward or not. Cons: less opportunity for peer support; some students may consistently not meet the expectations and, thus, not be motivated to participate.

All For One (interdependent group contingency)

Split the class into teams. Set a goal for the number of points needed to earn during your chosen activity in order to earn the reward. Every student on a team has to meet that goal in order for the whole team to win the reward. You could also set this up as Students vs. Teachers, where the students are all on one team and try to reach the set goal of "beating the teacher." You can see this visualized later in this chapter. Pros: builds positive teamwork skills as peers will be more motivated to support each other in engaging in the expected behaviors. Cons: if one student is not motivated by the reward, they could potentially "sabotage" their team by not attempting to meet the goal, resulting in no one on the team earning the reward.

One For All (dependent group contingency)

Split the class into teams. Set a goal for the number of points needed to earn during your chosen activity in order to earn the reward. On each team, only one student needs to meet this goal in order for the whole team to earn the reward. You can choose this student in advance (called "the hero procedure"), set it up that any student could win the reward for their team, or choose a "mystery student" by randomly drawing a student's name at the end of the activity and determining if that student earned the reward for the class. Pros: enables you to choose specific students you want to target for improved behaviors and gives opportunities for peers to support that student in meeting their goal. Cons: it's likely that some students will earn rewards without engaging in any expected behaviors.

Variations that could be added to any of the above three variations
- Mystery number: the number of how many points to earn is not revealed to the students. This prevents them from stopping engaging in the expected behaviors once they know they have earned the reward. If choosing this variation, it's recommended that you "mysteriously" pick a low number to start with, enabling more students to earn the reward on the first day.
- Mystery motivator: the teacher writes down a "mystery" reward that the students who meet the expectations will earn and places this paper in a box or bag somewhere visible to the students. The idea is that the reward will feel extra special and motivating because it could be anything!

Check-In, Check-Out

This strategy is intended to be used with an individual student in an inclusive setting. Some students may benefit from more one-on-one support throughout the day, reminding them of expectations and opportunities to earn rewards. Besides individualizing the expectations, there are other variations you can adjust to make this system better support your particular student, including choosing small rewards or breaks earned at each check-in time instead of earning an end-of-day reward.

Tips
- Ensure that the check-in times are set on a schedule where the student often earns their reward (start easy!).
- Check-ins should be less than one minute.
- Avoid using subjective terms like "You did well," "You're having a hard time," or "Today was not a good day." Instead, use the language that matches the expectations, such as, "You used kind words this morning!" or "You were not safe at circle time."

- If expectations were not met or rewards were not earned, use supportive language to provide feedback on what could be improved next time. Remind them when they can try again.
- Identify a discrete area for check-ins, as this feedback meeting should be private between you and your student.
- The first contact is pivotal in setting the tone for the day and, therefore, should be positive.
- Each day, the student "starts fresh," so use the first check-in to remind them of their expectations and give a little confidence boost.
- This strategy is especially effective for students who are engaging in challenging behaviors to seek attention or connection from others, as we are creating scheduled times to provide that attention proactively.

Individual Points Plan

Like the Check-In, Check-Out strategy, the Individual Points Plan is beneficial for use with an individual student in an inclusive setting. The family, teacher, and student should collaborate to determine the student's long-term academic and behavioral goals and what impedes the student from making progress toward those goals. What makes this strategy unique is its adaptability for students of all ages and its ability to promote independence.

Variations
- For younger students, this point system could look like a sticker chart where specific skills are identified and teachers fill up the student's board throughout the day as these skills are observed. For older students, tally marks to represent the points are more age-appropriate.
- Teachers can discretely award points as they walk around the classroom, reducing the amount that this student stands out as needing additional support. In comparison, for students who enjoy recognition, teachers could announce more publically when points are earned.
- To target more independence in self-monitoring skills, students can be taught to give themselves points for engaging in the target skills. Teachers can choose to do random checks for honesty if this is a concern.

Regardless of which reward strategy you choose for your students, remember to keep the rewards motivating and attainable. It's best practice never to remove points that have been earned. This can cause students to lose interest and not trust the system or the teacher. Instead, it's all about positively supporting students and celebrating their progress!

Building Rapport

Creating and maintaining positive relationships with students

Goal

Establish a genuine, trusting relationship that is the foundation of everything.

How

Dedicate time to get to know students' changing interests and motivations, engaging with them in activities they enjoy. **This is not a time for teaching, but rather "connection-building."**

Context

Building rapport should be a continuous effort made by all who support the student, including teachers, paraprofessionals, service providers, and family members. This approach may look different across the ages, but it is always an essential. It could also be beneficial for teachers to set up opportunities for students with similar interests to build rapport together.

Tip

Take time to learn about your students' special interests. This can help you more genuinely connect with them.

Recommended Guidelines for Building Rapport

- <u>Respect Boundaries:</u> Avoid being intrusive; strive to understand and engage with their world without imposing. For some students, it might be better for you to play nearby and wait for them to naturally approach you or invite you to join in.
- <u>Follow Their Lead:</u> Allow the student to guide the conversation or activity, showing interest in their preferences and choices.
- <u>Prioritize Comments Over Questions:</u> Asking a question and expecting them to answer is a demand, even when the question is about their interests. Instead, make comments about the activity to show engagement with no pressure for them to respond.
- <u>Allocate Time:</u> Research shows that just five minutes a day can lead to better student/teacher relationships.
- <u>Narrate Activities:</u> Describe what they are doing using their level and mode of communication as a natural teaching opportunity.
- <u>Remain Flexible:</u> Adapt to their changing interests moment by moment to allow them to continue leading the activity.

3 years old

6 years old

13 years old

19 years old

First, Then

Using a simple, structured statement to build motivation

Goal

Increase motivation in completing non-preferred tasks.

How

Identify a reward that will likely be motivating for the student (e.g. time on electronics, playing with a favorite toy, time with a friend, etc.). Make a statement in the form: "first (target task), then (reward)." Only give the reward once the student has completed the target task.

Context

This easy-to-use phrase can be inserted throughout the day with a variety of tasks. Before giving a demand, think if you can re-word it using a "first, then" phrase.

Tip

If at any time the student needs to take a break away from the task or engage in self-regulation skills, honor and support that. When they're ready to return, re-present the "First, Then" statement to remind them of the expectation and available reward.

You could also try blending this strategy with Firm, but Flexible to avoid power struggles!

You can find a sample First, Then board with illustrated icons in our Tools chapter!

Give instruction using "first, then"

State the target task followed by the reward that the student will earn. Choose a reward that will likely be motivating to them or have them choose!

Follow through

Follow through with the instruction by restating the "first, then" phrase to remind them of the motivation as needed. Remember, provide praise as they're completing the task!

Reward

Following the completion of the task, immediately provide the student with the reward that was promised. This is a good opportunity for you to join in too!

Providing Choices

Building engagement and empowerment through autonomy

Goal

By offering choices and fostering autonomy, students are more likely to feel motivated and remain engaged in their tasks.

How

Provide options within lesson activities, like letting students select their preferred way to demonstrate understanding, choose their workspace, decide on group partners, or determine the order of tasks. This empowers students to control their daily expectations and learning process, often leading to increased engagement and enjoyment in learning.

Context

This approach is beneficial across all grade levels, academic subjects, and school settings. Teachers can carefully select and offer choices that meet the educational goals while allowing students to exercise autonomy and engage with the material in a way that resonates with them.

Tip

Encourage students to reflect on how their choices impact their learning, helping them recognize their preferred learning methods and advocate for them effectively.

Limit the choices, limit student engagement

Choice of time

Other Ways to Provide Choices

- Choice of materials to use
- By yourself or with help
- Order of tasks
- Amount of work
- How to demonstrate understanding

Choice of location

Choice of who to work with

Whole Class Reward System

Building and rewarding better classroom behaviors

Goal

Build specific skills for the whole group during a typical teaching lesson.

How

Set and teach three to five defined classwide expectations relating to skills that you want to build. Have your students share ideas for rewards to earn, then split them up into teams, and choose an activity that your students struggle with the most. Give points for following expectations; the group with most points wins!

Context

Use this strategy when you can clearly identify the hardest part of your day (e.g. read-alouds, small groups, walking in the halls). Whole class reward systems are helpful for students of all ages and in any setting.

Tip

Try using an app like Class DoJo to electronically track points. The students can create their own characters to engage them even further. Another tip is to utilize student helpers who can help with recognizing peers who are engaging in the expected behaviors and assisting the teacher in giving out points. Research shows that this helps recognize and reward positive behaviors but also reduces challenging behaviors in the student helpers, as they are busy with their assigned job!

Set expectations

Choose one to three positively-worded behavior expectations for the entire class. Introduce the expectations to the students and hang up a visual in front of the class.

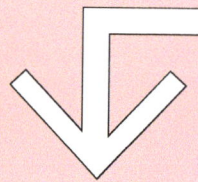

Choose activity

Identify the specific activity or lesson where challenging behaviors frequently occur. In this classroom, disruptive behavior is most common during small group and partner work.

Identify rewards

Ask for the students' input on rewards that can be earned. Provide guidance on what is feasible.

Determine teams

Choose a type of whole class reward system and split the class into teams accordingly (see chapter intro text). Here, the teacher is doing Teacher vs. Students where all the students are on one team together.

Legend

⇒ Teacher preparation
→ Student positive behavior

Play!

Each day during this particular activity, give points to students or teams who engage in the target expectations. Here, this teacher is giving the students a point anytime the whole class is following the expectations. He'll give the teacher a point when he needs to give a whole-class reminder.

Reward

When students or teams have met the expectations, they win the chosen reward!

3 Reward Options

Three approaches to improving one behavior

Goal

Select a reward strategy that best aligns with the team's top priority.

How

Collaboratively determine the team's priority goal: building communication and self-advocacy, teaching tolerance, or maintaining safety. Deciding which goal is the current biggest need guides the decision of which reward option to choose.

Context

Choosing a reward option is often part of the development of a student's Behavior Intervention Plan (BIP). Use this visual to help determine the team's top priority; then follow the guidelines for which reward strategy aligns. Describe what the strategy looks like for your particular student in their BIP.

Tip

You can always start with one; then once your goal is met, move to another! For example, if the student has limited communication skills, start with DRA. Once they've learned to consistently communicate their wants and needs, you could move to DRI where they learn to tolerate when what they requested is not available. Another example is if your student is engaging in high rates of dangerous behaviors at school (even though they have strong communication skills), you could first start with a DRO to aim to reduce that behavior from happening, and then move to a DRI to target their engagement in academic activities.

Challenging behavior scenario

In this example scenario, the student frequently (about every 15 minutes) engages in aggression toward teachers when expected to do academic tasks (function: escape).

Next, the team would meet to determine the priority goal. Based on this, they then choose one of the reward strategies to include in the behavior plan for the entire team to consistently implement. No matter which reward option they choose, initially, they should reward every success. Over time, they can fade out this reward, but at the beginning, consistent rewards will lead to faster progress!

Priority

Building communication & self-advocacy

Here, the goal is to build a behavior that is a better way for them to access or express their wants and needs. This behavior matches the function of the challenging behavior, meaning it's just a better way for them to get what they want or need. This often looks like recognizing their engagement in communication skills like asking for a break (as illustrated here), help, space, more time, items/ activities, or attention by rewarding them with exactly what they asked for.

Teaching tolerance

Here, we are aiming to build a specific expectation. This often involves tolerating something they may not particularly want to do, but need to do, including arriving to class on time, taking turns, completing assignments, and following directions. The team will choose one specific behavior to build and then determine a reward that the student can earn for engaging in this specific expected behavior.

Maintaining safety

Here, our focus is on reducing the challenging behavior by rewarding times that it did not occur. The student does not have to engage in any specific behavior to earn the reward. First, determine how often the behavior is occurring, and then create a schedule where the student can earn a reward for going a specific amount of time (just less than their baseline) without engaging in the challenging behavior. Here, although the student is not completing any assignments, she hasn't had aggression in ten minutes, so she'll earn the reward.

Token Boards

Using visuals to create clear expectations and track progress toward rewards

Goal

Build motivation and patience by visually tracking progress toward a goal.

How

Identify one or two skills that you want to teach or promote. Then, determine what items or activities can be earned. Create rules for how tokens can be earned and when they can be exchanged for the reward. Make adjustments over time as needed, such as increasing the number of tokens needed to earn the reward. Token boards should be used for more short-term teaching of new skills and then faded out to more natural ways of recognizing and celebrating progress.

Context

Token boards are commonly used with younger students. For older students, try the Individual Points Plan instead. When choosing which behaviors or skills to give tokens for, choose ones that the student already knows how to do but they just need more motivation to do it more often or consistently.

Tips

- Ask for the student's input on rewards they'd like to earn. This will increase the motivation to work for them!
- Try making a customized token board with the student's favorite characters as faces instead of stars.
- We've included two token boards in the Tools chapter.
- Make sure that the student is earning the reward often enough for it to stay motivating.

Set up

Determine the rules for the token board, and teach them to the student.

Encourage independence

While we should be nearby and ready to give tokens as needed, it's also important to give the student space and opportunities to be independent.

Introduce

Remind the student what expectation earns a token, as well as what reward he is trying to earn.

Recognize & reward

As they engage in the target expected behavior, give token and specific praise. Eventually, you will fade out the token board altogether and just keep the praise.

Legend
⇒ Teacher preparation
→ Student positive behavior

Timing the reward

When possible, space out the delivery of the tokens so that the board is full at the same time the class is taking a natural transition or break.

Reward

Give the reward as soon as the token board is full, joining in with them if they like that. The token board will then be cleared and ready to use again.

Range of Rewards

Rewarding efforts

Goal

Recognize and celebrate big efforts to create motivation for those efforts to continue.

How

For an individual student, determine what are low, medium, and big effort tasks or instructions. Create a clear plan for providing corresponding sizes of rewards.

Context

This strategy is best for individual students who have a particular task or instruction that is frequently challenging for them. That way, when they do engage in this skill, we will be prepared to recognize and celebrate them!

Tip

Encourage all teachers who support this student to follow this same structured reward plan, as consistency is key!

Legend
→ Student positive behavior

Low effort, little reward

When building a new skill like following directions, it's important to recognize and reward all attempts and progress. Here, participating is usually easy for this student, so the paraprofessional is giving her one star.

Medium effort, medium reward

As the student engages in tasks that are somewhat challenging to them, continue to recognize and reward. It's also helpful if all teachers are involved! Here, the teacher is giving two stars for being on task.

Big effort, big reward

Some tasks or instructions can be especially difficult for students. When they do this skill independently, that's worth celebrating! Here, this paraprofessional is giving five stars for the student pressing pause when asked.

Check-In, Check-Out

Frequent feedback meetings throughout the day

Goal

Improve a specific student's behaviors by giving scheduled reminders of expectations, encouragement, and feedback.

How

Determine one to three positively-worded behavior expectations specifically for the student. Set the schedule based on how often they are engaging in challenging behaviors. Collaborate with the family and student to identify motivating rewards. At the morning check-in, the trusted staff will remind the student what behaviors will earn their chosen reward and provide encouragement to start their day. At the scheduled check-ins throughout the day, the trusted staff will review progress and provide feedback. Rewards will be given at the predetermined time: at set times during the school day, at the end of the day, or at home.

Context

This strategy is helpful for individual students who exhibit consistent challenging behaviors throughout the school day. It's especially effective for students who value adult connection, as they will be having brief one-on-one interactions throughout the day.

Tip

Build independence with accountability by having the student reflect on if they earned their points or not during each check-in. You can also decide to give bonus rewards for honesty when introducing this expectation.

Set up

Set expectations

Choose one to three positively-worded behavior expectations specific to this student. Introduce the system by teaching them these daily expectations. Use the visual provided in the Tools chapter.

Introduce

Remember, your goals are to be safe, ask for help, and use kind words. I know you can do it!

Check-in

At the beginning of each school day and at the scheduled check-in times, a trusted staff will remind the student about the expectations and rewards, offering encouragement for their day ahead.

2

Set schedule

Determine how often the target challenging behavior is occurring (about every x minutes). Set up your check-in schedule to have feedback meetings just a little bit prior (e.g. set your meetings to occur every 30 minutes if the behaviors happen about every 35 minutes).

3

I know that you love playing basketball. Are there other activities you'd like to earn at the end of the day?

Set rewards

Collaborate with the family and student to identify motivating rewards. The team may choose to give smaller rewards throughout the day (at check-in times) or a bigger reward at the end of the day (at school or at home).

Legend
⇒ Teacher preparation
→ Student positive behavior

5

I love that you asked for help when you and your friend were arguing. This helped you stay safe today!

Check-out

During the scheduled check-ins throughout the day, the teacher and student will review together if the student followed the expectations during that previous period. At the end of the day, they will review the whole day's behavior and determine if the reward was earned.

6

Reward

When the reward is earned, it should be given right away. This is a great opportunity for the trusted staff to join in too!

Individual Points Plan

Discrete individual support
to build motivation

Goal

Build specific skills for a student by recognizing and rewarding these behaviors.

How

Establish a long-term goal and consider their current levels of skills needed to meet this goal. Determine one to three specific skills that will help the student achieve the long-term goal. Collaborate with the student to determine rewards and how many points are needed to earn each reward. Throughout the day, discretely give points when the student engages in the target skills. Once the target number of points are earned, the student receives the reward.

Context

This strategy is helpful for individual students who struggle with motivation to complete standard academic and behavior expectations. Because there is not much time requirement for teachers, this strategy is a good choice for students in general education who need a little extra support. Students will need to be able to tolerate waiting for their rewards for this strategy to be effective.

Tip

If the student has not earned enough points to earn a reward within the first three days, adjust the points plan to make it more attainable by changing either the amount of points needed or when the rewards are given (e.g. end of day vs. half day).

Determine skills

As a whole team, determine the student's current behavioral and academic concerns at school.

Determine rewards

Collaborate with the student to determine rewards and how many points are needed to earn each reward. Provide feedback on what is feasible and attainable. To be most effective, set up the system where the student will likely earn rewards right away (start easy and build up!).

2

Present level

Identify what you can track to determine progress toward meeting the student's long-term goals (e.g. graduating). Record where the student is currently at so that you can later determine if this strategy was effective.

3

Arriving to class on time

Participating in class

Turning in assignments

Determine points plan

As a team, determine one to three specific skills that will help the student achieve the long-term goal. Here, this team has chosen to target the skills of arriving to class on time, participating in class, and turning in assignments.

Legend

⇒ Teacher preparation
→ Student positive behavior

5

Introduce

Review expectations with the student as necessary. Award points discreetly throughout the day for demonstrating target skills. Consider using a secret signal to indicate points earned, allowing the student to self-record. The teacher initials at the end of each class to agree.

6

Reward

Once the student earns the predetermined number of points, they earn the reward! You can choose to set it up where they can earn a reward each day or the points are cumulative toward earning a bigger reward.

Preventing Challenging Behaviors

Introduction

The more we can prevent, the less we need to manage!

As a behavior expert, the most common question is, "What do I do when ... occurs?" Instead of placing the focus on how to respond, we should shift the focus to how to better set that student up for success. There are two types of "antecedent" strategies, or strategies that we do proactively: Preventative strategies, which you'll find in this chapter, and Teaching strategies, which you'll find in the next chapter. They're both essential for reducing those challenging behaviors that you're concerned about.

Most of us organize and simplify our lives, such as creating to-do lists, utilizing daily/weekly planners, and incorporating breaks into our workdays. Individuals with Autism and other developmental disorders may require assistance in managing frustrating situations and how to better prepare for them. The proactive strategies in the following chapter have all proven to be effective at improving skills, motivation, and behavior, but you'll need to find which works best for you and your student!

Prevention starts before students even step foot in school! It begins with classroom set-up. In this chapter, we've illustrated examples of different ways you can promote inclusive learning and proactively set your student's environment up to support them best. Also, see Understanding and Celebrating Neurodiversity for more tips on inclusive classroom setup.

When thinking about which preventative strategy to use, we recommend first thinking of what are the most common triggers.

Strategy Recommendations for Common Triggers
- Transitions: Priming, Easy, Easy, Hard, and Visual Schedule
- Tolerating "no": A Better Way to Say "No"
- Presenting academic tasks: Easy, Easy, Hard, Class Pass, and Scheduled Breaks

If there's one situation that's particularly hard for your student, try the Power Card strategy! While lesser-known, it's incredibly user-friendly. Rather than crafting a full social story, you simply create a brief visual guide outlining expectations and review it with them before the challenging situation. Best of all, it's tailored to your student's unique interests!

Realistically, you may need to combine multiple preventative strategies to best set your students up for success. You may also be using some of the strategies from the previous chapter to build motivation before even preparing them for a difficult instruction or situation. This can feel intimidating at first, so we recommend starting with one and building on it as you feel comfortable. We recommend starting with the following strategies, which are user-friendly and offer versatility for a wide range of students and situations.

Strategy Recommendations to Try First

- Classroom Set-up
- Building Rapport (previous chapter)
- Providing Choices (previous chapter)
- Priming

Preventative strategies can be done classwide or with individual students. If you're looking for strategies to support individual students, try any of the strategies found in this chapter! They can all be adjusted for individual needs - you can read more about that within the How/Context/Tip text described in the visual strategies. For ideas on integrating preventive strategies into your classroom teaching, consider the following strategies:

Strategy Recommendations for a Classwide Approach

- Classroom Set-up
- Priming
- Easy, Easy, Hard
- Visual schedule
- Scheduled breaks

Classroom Setup

An inclusive environment for all

Goal

Create a classroom where all students' needs can be easily met.

How

At the start of the year, design your classroom setup thoughtfully in consideration of students with diverse needs. Use the example classroom illustrated as inspiration. As you meet and get to know each of your students, adjust your classroom setup further to better meet their individual needs.

Context

Creating a purposeful and inclusive classroom environment is essential for all classrooms, not just those designated for special education. This includes incorporating visuals, offering alternative seating choices, and designating spaces for sensory and emotional regulation throughout every learning environment.

Tip

When deciding which visual supports to use, consider your students' age and developmental levels over aesthetic design. For example, illustrations are symbolic, and some students may benefit more from actual pictures. Also, plain, simple text is often easier to read than cursive for many students.

Designated calm corner with visual supports and calming activities

Visual cues to help with classroom routines and expectations

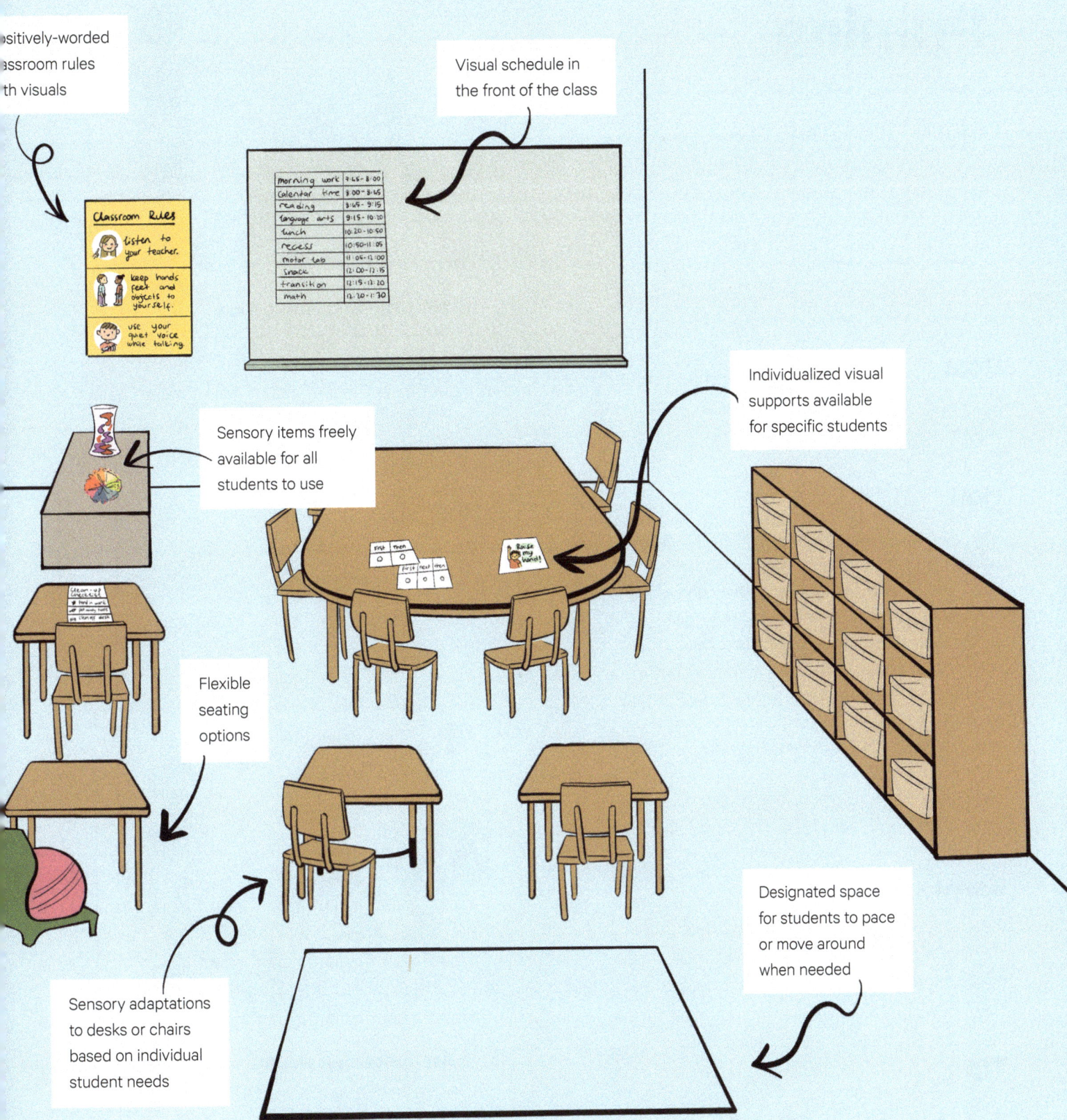

Positively-worded classroom rules with visuals

Visual schedule in the front of the class

Individualized visual supports available for specific students

Sensory items freely available for all students to use

Flexible seating options

Sensory adaptations to desks or chairs based on individual student needs

Designated space for students to pace or move around when needed

Priming

Preparing students in advance

Goal

Increase student success with an upcoming activity or event by preparing them for it in advance.

How

Prior to a situation that may be difficult for one student or all students, the teacher will inform the student(s) about what is upcoming. This can be through the use of a time countdown ("Five minutes until we clean up") or a verbal reminder of expectations prior to a new situation ("We have an assembly this afternoon"). Priming can also be used in the classroom by showing students the materials and demonstrating what to do prior to asking them to complete a new task.

When preparing your student(s) for an upcoming event, remind them to use their coping skills if needed.

Context

- Transitions
- Changes in schedule
- New situations
- Starting a task

Tip

You can use a visual schedule like the one found in our Tools chapter to prime students about what to expect each day.

No prime, less success

By immediately presenting the difficult event (lining up), student(s) may have little success with following through.

An upcoming event

Teacher will recognize that an upcoming event may be difficult for the student(s).

After prime, more success

Following the prime, the students are more likely to have success during the difficult event, as they were prepared for what was coming.

In one minute, it's time to line up.

Give prime (immediately prior)

Remind the student(s) of the upcoming expectation just prior to the possibly difficult event.

When the big hand is on the red line, it's time to clean up and line up.

Give prime (in advance)

Give student(s) a prime in advance: either five minutes before a transition, or at the beginning of the school day.

Power Card

Personalized, visual reminder

Goal

Prevent challenging behaviors in a specific situation by providing an individualized reminder.

How

First, identify the student's interests. Create a personalized visual card featuring their favorite character following one to three specific expectations for that challenging situation. Then, just prior to that situation, present and review the card with them using an encouraging and supportive tone.

Context

This strategy is beneficial for individual students who frequently engage in challenging behavior during a specific task, situation, or activity. It's similar to a social story, but it's more targeted.

Tip

While this strategy has been shown to be beneficial for many students, it may not be the best choice for students who think more literally. For example, in this illustration, the student may interpret the card to mean, "act like a dinosaur," which is not the intention of this strategy. For those students, providing explicit expectations could be better.

A challenging behavior

A specific situation in which a student commonly engages in challenging behavior. Here, this student frequently has aggression on the playground.

Create the Power Card

Consider your student's special interests. Design a visual featuring that interest as a character who is following one to three specific expectations.

Better behaviors

Following this personalized, visual reminder, the student is more likely to have better behaviors in this situation.

Present the Power Card

Just prior to that commonly challenging situation, review the visual with the student, encouraging them to follow the expectations.

Official title: High probability, low probability sequence that creates behavior momentum

Easy, Easy, Hard

Building momentum
in starting a task

Goal

Student(s) will improve with task initiation.

How

Increase students' motivation and engagement in starting a non-preferred task by starting with two back-to-back tasks that the students are easily able to complete. Then, when you give the difficult task, the students are already engaging in a pattern of following instructions. You are helping them get started; then by the time the difficult task is presented, they're already on a roll!

Context

This strategy can be used individually or classwide and for a wide variety of tasks. Consider which tasks are the hardest for your student(s) to get started (e.g. getting off electronics, transitioning back to the classroom, etc.). Then think of what easy instructions you could start with just prior to giving this tricky one!

Tip

When choosing easy tasks to give, make them related to the target task.

For example, if the target task is to attend to a book being read at circle time, first you could say "let's hop to our spots" (easy task), "point to the book we're going to read" (easy task). Now, when you are ready to start the "hard" activity ("time to listen"), the students are already attending.

No initiation

By immediately presenting a difficult task, the student(s) may feel overwhelmed, resulting in difficulty in initiating the task.

First easy task

Start with a simple task that the student(s) can easily complete.

Initiating hard task

Build on the momentum by presenting the difficult task immediately following success with the easier tasks. If they follow the instruction, make sure to reward them at this step.

Second easy task

Continue by immediately giving another easy task to complete.

A Better Way to Say "No"

Two approaches for responding when something is unavailable

Goal

Prevent challenging behaviors that typically arise when something is unavailable.

How

Hearing "no" or "wait" is diffcult for many students! Researchers evaluated different ways to say "no" or "wait" to determine which would result in the least challenging behaviors. They identified two successful approaches: "No + alternative" and "Yes, when..." Try switching up how you say "no" by using one of these sentence structures to respond! Interestingly, saying "no" + giving the rationale why something is unavailable at the moment was not successful at preventing challenging behaviors.

Context

Practice responding with one or both of these approaches if hearing "no" or "wait" is a common trigger for challenging behaviors for your student.

Tip

To teach your student to practice tolerating "no," you could set up a role-play situation in which you tell the student to make a request, but tell them in advance you're going to say "no." Instruct them to practice saying "ok" and choosing another activity to do. If they do this, immediately celebrate it by giving the item they initially requested. Over time, you can fade out the role-plays and the big celebrations, but still remember to praise them, as this is a tricky skill across the ages!

Question

The student asks for something that is not available right now or at all (the answer is "no" or "wait").

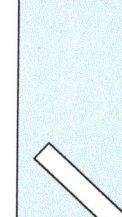

No + alternative

When saying "no," provide two alternative options.

Accepts alternative

Research shows that when a student is provided an alternative option, they are less likely to engage in challenging behaviors following the "no" response.

Yes, when...

If the student can have what they are requesting, but just at a later time, respond with "yes, when... (when it is available)."

Waits

Research shows that when a student is told "yes, when...", they they are less likely to engage in the challenging behaviors that follow the "no" response.

Visual Schedule

Building predictability through visuals

Goal

Create structure and predictability in daily activities to build independence and minimize challenging behaviors.

How

First, determine the order of the activities occurring that day, starting with times that are locked in and then adding in a blend of structured and unstructured activities to fill the day. Don't forget to save time for scheduled breaks! Next, the teacher should place the visual schedule where students can easily see it throughout the day. Review the schedule at the start of the day, and refer to it during transitions. We have a visual schedule for you to use in the Tools chapter!

Context

Schedules are helpful for everyone! While illustrations with text are helpful for younger students, older students would benefit more from text with specific times listed. Consider what is the best style for your particular students.

Tip

When moving to the next activity on the schedule, build student independence in moving through routines by having them move the activity to a "done" column or telling the class what's next on the schedule.

1

Set the schedule

Arrange the day's activities in order, beginning with fixed times and then including a mix of structured and unstructured tasks.

4

Rebecca, please move "circle time" to "done."

Invite student involvement

Throughout the day, draw your student's attention to the visual schedule to help them become familiarized with the classroom routines.

Post the schedule

Place the visual schedule where students can easily see it throughout the day.

Introduce the schedule

Review the schedule at the start of each day, emphasizing any changes to your typical schedule. This may be a good opportunity to proactively practice self-regulation skills, as a change in schedule may be difficult for some students.

Legend

⇒ Teacher preparation

Promote student independence

Encourage students to refer to the schedule during transitions to help them become more independent in following routines.

Break Tickets

Promoting self-management with break tickets

Goal

Improve self-management and prevent challenging behaviors.

How

First, determine about how many times per day the student engages in work avoidance. Add one or two to this and that's how many break tickets you'll give them! Students can decide when to exchange these tickets for a break, fostering self-awareness and self-regulation. Unused break tickets at the end of the day can be traded for free time or a reward, motivating engagement throughout the day. You can lessen the amount of tickets given over time.

Context

This strategy is beneficial for individual students, as the number of breaks students may need varies. Given that students must manage their tickets and exercise self-awareness, it may be more advantageous for older students.

Tip

It is recommended that the teacher still include scheduled breaks for all students within their classroom schedule.

1

Work avoidance

A student engages in work avoidance behaviors throughout the day, even though you've tried embedding their interests and choices into the lessons.

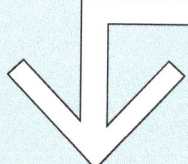

4

Accept tickets

Allow all student requests to use a break ticket and remind them of the break expectations.

2

Determine need

Calculate the average number of times the student engages in these behaviors throughout the day.

3

You have six break tickets you can use at any time. A ticket gets you 5 minutes of a drawing or reading break.

Introduce tickets

Calculate the number of tickets for the student by adding one or two to their average. Next, provide clear instructions on how to use the tickets, specifying what they can be exchanged for, such as the duration of the break and available activities.

Legend

⇒ Teacher preparation
→ Student positive behavior
→ Student challenging behavior

5

Structured break

The student engages in the designated break activities and sets a timer. You may need to go back to Step 2 to adjust the amount of tickets or length of breaks.

6

End of day exchange

Unused break tickets at the end of the day can be traded for free time or a reward, motivating engagement throughout the day.

Official title: Noncontingent reinforcement

Scheduled Breaks/ Connections

Filling their cups

Goal

Proactively meet the diverse sensory-needs of students.

How

Recognizing our students' diverse needs, we should allocate specific times for movement, calmness, and social interaction. This approach "fills their cups" by proactively addressing sensory and social-emotional needs, reducing the likelihood that students will seek out these needs during structured academic periods.

Context

Although these breaks will look different across the ages, we all need breaks throughout the day!

Tip

When determining how often to schedule your breaks, consider that the average attention span of a neurotypical student is two to three times their age. That's a good guideline for how often these brief breaks should be happening!

Scheduled Movement Breaks

Scheduled Movement Breaks

Scheduled Calm Breaks

Teaching New Skills

Introduction

Written in collaboration with Nadia Guajardo, M. Ed, BCBA

The best learning happens when students are happy, relaxed, and engaged. If we teach when students are calm, when those challenging moments arise, we can more effectively support them by reminding them of the skills they've been practicing. Behavioral skills need to be taught just like academics! We can't expect students to know how to effectively communicate, self-regulate, or problem-solve without giving them the tools and strategies they need. Repetitive practice is key when it comes to teaching behavioral skills. Just like learning a new math concept, students need multiple opportunities to practice and refine their skills in order for them to become fluent and efficient.

As teachers, we excel at creating teachable moments. Let's use this same strength and skillset to create opportunities to teach social-emotional and behavioral skills, too! Whether contrived or naturally occurring, these scenarios serve as valuable chances to teach new self-management and coping skills. For instance, if a student struggles with handling mistakes, teaching self-regulation or problem-solving skills can help them cope with frustration proactively. Instead of erasing their worksheet until every pencil mark vanishes, tearing the paper, crumpling it into a ball, stomping over to the trash can, throwing it away, and even kicking the trash can, they could simply ask for a new worksheet. They can then pause, take a breath, and start again.

Throughout the day, we have the chance to create teachable moments. For example, while writing on the whiteboard, we can deliberately "make a mistake" and model taking a deep breath and talking aloud (e.g., "I can stop, take a breath, and start over. Everyone makes mistakes sometimes, and that's okay."). In these contrived practice opportunities, we may role-play, make a mistake, and use the coping strategy to stay calm. Then, when real-life mistakes happen, we can view this as an opportunity to help them proactively use their coping strategy before they resort to challenging behaviors. Either way, teaching is always proactive!

Teaching vs. Supporting

Teaching is proactive and should happen when students are happy, relaxed, and engaged. Supporting is how we respond, reminding and helping them do the new skill.

By understanding the difference between teaching and supporting, we can better meet our students' needs. Teaching is more contrived, structured, and planned, while supporting is more in-the-moment and responsive; however, both are necessary to help students learn new skills.

It's important to recognize when a student may need teaching vs support. If they are struggling with a specific skill, it may be time for some dedicated teaching time. This can involve breaking down the skill into smaller steps and providing visual aids or prompts. In this chapter, we've illustrated different methods for teaching new skills. When choosing which to use, consider how your student learns best!

How Do We Teach?

- Modeling
- Shaping
- Fading
- Breaking Down Skills
- Choice Mapping

What Do We Teach?

When deciding on skills to teach in hopes of promoting better student behaviors, there are three essentials: communication, self-regulation, and executive functioning. For most students, these should be taught in a hierarchy, where we first prioritize helping them learn to express themselves, then how to use coping strategies to manage frustrations, and finally how to build skills that will help them succeed, including inhibitory control, shift, emotional control, working memory, and planning/organization. However, as with everything, choosing what to teach and how we teach it is completely individualized based on the student's current needs.

Communication

It's essential to make sure that every student, regardless of their mode of communication, has the opportunity to express their desires, needs, thoughts, and ideas. This ensures that all students have a voice. Tailoring communication instruction to each student is key. Collaborating with their Speech Language Pathologist (SLP) and Board Certified Behavior Analyst (BCBA) can help pinpoint the communication mode, words, phrases, and teaching strategies that are best based on the student's learning style, strengths, and preferences.

Here, we're teaching students the importance and effectiveness of using words to express their needs, rather than resorting to challenging behaviors. Phrases like "I need help," "I need a break," or "I need space" can have a significant impact, and it's crucial to respect and acknowledge these requests. These phrases are often incorporated as alternative skills in a student's Behavior Intervention Plan (BIP). When the goal is to empower students with a way to communicate their needs instead of displaying challenging behaviors, it's referred to as Functional Communication Training (FCT).

In a recent research study involving over 100 children with developmental delays and destructive behaviors, simply teaching them better ways to communicate their needs resulted in a remarkable 90% reduction in challenging behaviors. This strategy is powerful! If you are including FCT as part of a student's BIP, it's essential to have a clear plan outlining the instructions for teaching these phrases. For guidance, please refer to the "Teaching to Request" visual strategy on page 166.

Remember, communication is not just about teaching requests. Partner with your SLP or AAC Specialist to learn how to teach language that will give the student more opportunity to express themselves throughout the day or be more included with peers. See our book, *AAC Visualized*, to learn more!

Visual Strategies that Teach Communication Skills

- Introducing Communication
- Teaching to Request
- Building Better Behaviors
- Self-Advocacy

Self-Regulation

Self-regulation is the ability to control and manage your emotions as well as your reactions to your emotions. This includes when you have them, how you experience them, and how you express or act on them. Emotional regulation is important because it keeps us within our optimal zone, or "The Window of Tolerance." The Window of Tolerance was coined by Dr. Dan Siegel, and it's since been adopted to understand our emotions. The zone of tolerance can be described as the perfect window where we aren't overstimulated or overwhelmed and we aren't understimulated or underwhelmed. Everyone has their unique zone of tolerance where they can experience different emotions and remain within the zone or a regulated state. Here you can think clearly, process information, and do what you need to do, so it's the ideal state to be in. Self-regulation represents a significant step toward independence and self-management and should be taught to students of all ages. For neurodiverse students, teaching these skills becomes even more essential, as they may have more difficulties with executive function and regulating emotions.

Classwide Strategies that Promote and Normalize Self-Regulation

- Calm Down Corners: One powerful tool for promoting self-regulation is having a designated space in the classroom that students can freely access when they need to regulate their emotions. To make this space more effective, establish clear guidelines for requesting and using it. For example, you can teach students a secret gesture they can use to signal that they need some time in the Calm Down Corner. Additionally, having a timer in the corner allows students to set their own time limit for calming down. After the timer goes off, encourage students to do a feelings check-in to assess if they are ready to rejoin the class or need more time. See a Calm Down Corner visualized in our Classroom Setup visual strategy.
- Sensory Activities: Another effective strategy for promoting self-regulation is offering students free access to sensory bins filled with fidget materials. These bins can contain various items such as stress balls, squishy toys, liquid motion toys, or other items that spark or calm the senses. Alternatively, some students may prefer to have specific sensory items available on or near their desks for easier access. Providing these resources allows students to independently utilize calming sensory tools whenever they feel the need, promoting their independent self-regulation. These sensory materials offer a valuable outlet for students to regulate their emotions, especially during times of feeling overwhelmed or overstimulated.

- Identifying Emotions Visuals: Visual aids are essential for teaching students about emotions and how to identify them in themselves and others. Use visuals such as emotion cards or charts displaying different facial expressions to help students recognize and label their feelings. This tool can be particularly helpful in helping students understand their emotions and communicate them effectively. If you have AAC users in class, show them where to find their emotions pages and model it frequently.
- Coping Skills Visuals: Another valuable tool for promoting self-regulation is creating visuals of coping skills that students can refer to when feeling distressed or anxious. Display images or posters illustrating coping strategies like deep breathing exercises, counting to ten, or taking a break in a designated quiet space such as a calm corner. By providing concrete visuals of these coping skills, you give students tangible ways to manage their emotions and behaviors effectively. See our "Coping Skills Visual Posters" in our Tools chapter.

By encouraging the use of these tools, teachers prepare students to manage their emotional well-being independently, thereby paving the way for success in the classroom and beyond. It is never too early or too late to teach these life skills!

Visual Strategies and Tools that Teach Self-Regulation Skills
- Self-Regulation
- Calming Tools Visual Poster
- 5-4-3-2-1 Calm Visual Poster
- Sensory-Supportive Environment Template

Executive Functioning

Once students demonstrate effective communication and self-regulation, we can introduce, teach, and reinforce executive functioning skills. These cognitive skills enable students to plan, organize, regulate emotions, and problem-solve effectively. While these skills are essential for all students, neurodiverse students may need additional support in developing and using them independently. In this chapter, you'll find an illustrated step-by-step guide to teaching Problem Solvin that can be used by students of all ages. For young learners, the five executive functioning domains to prioritize teaching are Inhibitory Control, Shift, Emotional Control, Working Memory, and Planning and Organization. These five areas help students control behavior and emotional responses, transition, focus on assigned tasks, and plan and complete pertinent tasks. Challenging behaviors may stem from limited executive functioning skills, which are not fully developed even in neurotypical young learners. As a teacher, it is important to use effective and compassionate strategies to support students in developing and strengthening these skills.

1. Inhibitory Control

Inhibitory control is a crucial skill for students, allowing them to stop impulses and respond appropriately, influencing social interactions like sharing and refraining from challenging behaviors. When sharing toys, students with inhibitory control may ask for a turn, while those lacking this skill may grab or act impulsively. A delay in inhibitory control can make sharing, waiting, and self-control difficult for young students, affecting their ability to choose between immediate and delayed rewards.

Try this!

One effective way to teach inhibitory control is through "Stop and Go" games. These games involve activities where students have to stop or go based on cues provided by the teacher or music. Dancing or singing with movements can make these games even more enjoyable for young students. For example, you can play the dance/freeze game where students dance when the music plays and freeze when it stops. Using props like a stop/go sign can also help reinforce the concept of inhibitory control. Repetition is key when teaching these games, as young students need practice to understand the concept of stopping impulses.

2. Shift

Shift refers to the ability to move freely from one situation, activity, or aspect of a problem to another as the circumstances demand. Key aspects of shifting include the ability to (a) make transitions; (b) tolerate change; (c) problem-solve flexibly; and (d) switch or alternate attention.

Try this!

Build attentional flexibility: Integrate engaging activities like scavenger hunts that require students to switch their focus between different tasks or materials. By practicing shifting attention between visual, auditory, or kinesthetic cues, students can enhance their ability to adapt and switch attention when necessary.

3. Emotional Control

Emotional control is the ability of a student to manage emotions and reactions in a healthy way, even when situations are challenging. Students who struggle with self-regulation might have trouble controlling their behaviors when they experience challenges or frustrations. It's important for teachers to support students in developing these skills by providing tools for self-soothing, helping them learn to shift their focus away from negative triggers, and setting goals that help them stay on track. Some students may need additional support from a trusted adult to help them learn how to manage their emotions effectively through co-regulation until they have developed the skills required to independently self-regulate. Review our self-regulation recommendations above if this is an area of need for your students.

4. Working Memory

As a teacher, you have the important responsibility of helping your students succeed academically. One key aspect of this is recognizing the role that working memory plays in their learning. Working memory is the ability to hold information in mind for a brief period of time in order to complete a task, encode information, or generate goals and plans.

In your classroom, you likely ask your students to follow a variety of directions throughout the day, ranging from simple one-step instructions to more complex multi-step directions. For students who struggle with working memory, following these directions can be a challenge. This can lead to frustration, confusion, and difficulty completing tasks. It's important to recognize that working memory is a skill that can be improved with practice and support. As a teacher, there are several strategies you can use to help your students develop and strengthen their working memory. For example, breaking down complex tasks into smaller, more manageable steps can make it easier for students to remember and follow directions. Additionally, providing visual aids or written instructions can be helpful for students who struggle with auditory processing.

<u>Try this!</u>
Use a mini-sequence (e.g. First/Then Sequence). This visual is a precursor to a longer visual schedule and is especially beneficial for students who may find a traditional visual schedule overwhelming. The mini-sequence shows only two pictures at a time, such as "first art, then recess" or "first circle time, then lunch." By providing a clear visual of what is coming next, students can process the information more effectively and keep it at the forefront of their minds. This way, they can refer back to the visual as many times as needed rather than relying solely on verbal instructions that disappear once spoken.

5. Plan & Organize

This domain encompasses the ability of students to effectively manage present and future task requirements within a given context. This involves setting clear goals and outlining the necessary steps to accomplish tasks or goals in advance. A student exhibiting difficulties in this area may struggle with planning and organizing information, materials, or actions required for successful task completion. They may require additional support and strategies to develop these skills and navigate tasks effectively.

<u>Try this!</u>
Break tasks into smaller steps: Guide students to learn how to break down complex tasks into manageable steps, using examples relevant to their assignments. Encourage them to create a checklist or timeline to track their progress and celebrate each completed step.

Modeling

I do, we do, you do

Goal

Teach a new skill with this structured 4-step approach.

How

1. Introduce the skill by explaining how to do it and its importance.
2. Demonstrate the skill in a relatable scenario.
3. Let students practice through role-play.
4. Give specific feedback on what they did well and ways to improve.

Context

In a recent study analyzing 118 research articles on methods for teaching new skills, this particular approach showed the most consistent improvement in skill development. You can use this approach with all students, whether individually or classwide.

Tip

For students who like to learn by reading instead of by watching, try an alternative teaching method called "the teach-back method."

1. Provide written instructions
2. Ask questions to check for understanding
3. Practice
4. Feedback

Legend

 Teacher preparation

Ways to Model

- Teacher Modeling: Teachers demonstrate the behavior or skill directly, providing clear examples for students to follow.
- Peer Modeling: Students learn from each other through observation and imitation in naturally occurring situations.
- Video Modeling: Using curated or created videos, students observe and learn specific behaviors or skills on their own.
- Animated Modeling: Animated characters or simulations act out scenes to teach the skills in a visually engaging way.

Explain

Clearly explain the skill to be taught and why it's valuable for students to learn.

Demonstrate

Show the skill in action using a relatable scenario, making it easy for students to understand and connect with.

Practice

Engage students in hands-on activities or role-playing exercises to allow them to actively apply the skill.

Feedback

Provide specific and constructive feedback on students' performance, highlighting strengths and areas for improvement.

Shaping

Building skills over time

Goal

Gradually improve a behavior or a skill.

How

Sometimes there's an expectation that's just too difficult for a student to do consistently right now. Using Shaping, we can make progress toward that skill by setting gradual goals that increasingly get closer to the end goal over time.

Context

This gradual approach to building skills can be used across a wide variety of skills including communication, amount of time engaged in a task, or refining fine motor skills like handwriting.

Tip

This is an ideal opportunity to foster neurodiversity-affirming acceptance in your classroom, as some may perceive it as "unfair" that one student has different expectations than others. However, it's important to recognize that each student is doing their best at their own pace, and by supporting them, we help them improve at their own speed.

Present level

When there is a skill you're wanting to build, we have to first consider what the student's present level is. Here, this student is not participating in circle time at all.

Continue building

Continue to gradually increase the difficulty of the student's expectation and reward them for their progress and efforts. Here, the student is now participating in circle time with the group!

Start building

To start, consider what expectation you could set that the student would be likely to meet at this time. Here, by giving this student a chair and a toy to hold, he's now attending to circle time.

Continue building

Gradually increase the difficulty of the student's expectation, rewarding them for their progress and efforts. Here, the student is still sitting a little away from the group in a chair, but he no longer has a toy.

Demonstrates target skill

Continue building and rewarding until the student has met the expectation and is consistently doing the skill. Here, the student is now leading the calendar activity at circle time.

Legend
⇒ Teacher preparation
→ Student positive behavior

Fading

Building independence
over time

Goal

Student independence!

How

Gradually reduce the amount of assistance provided
to allow the student to be more independent in
completing the skill. This is usually done over time, but
the rate is different student by student and skill by skill.
Here, we've illustrated one way to reduce prompts over
time, but this may look different for your student.

Context

Use this strategy when teaching a new skill. When
students are consistently following along with your
guidance of how to do the skill, it's time to start fading.
Our goal is always for students to be as independent as
possible.

Tip

When providing assistance, try to limit the amount of
verbal prompting (or instructing) you are providing, as
students may become dependent on these. Instead, try
using visuals, gestures, and teaching by showing.

Full support

When a student is learning a new skill, providing
full support can be beneficial at first. Here, the
teacher is physically helping the student with
his morning routine of hanging up his backpack.

Reducing support

Now the student is almost doing the skill by
themselves. Provide minimal support such as
a gesture or a visual.

Reducing support

As the student begins to follow along with your lead, reduce the level of support. Here, the teacher is tapping on the student's backpack strap as a hint to take it off.

Reducing support

Once the student is consistently doing the skill with that level of support, reduce support a little more. Here, the teacher is pointing toward the cubby as a reminder. If the student needs more support, you can always go back one step.

Independence

The student is now independently doing this skill! Continue to recognize and reward them until this becomes part of their typical routine.

Legend
→ Student positive behavior
→ Student may need more support

Breaking Down Skills

Teaching a multi-step skill

Goal

Teach a new, complex skill by breaking it down into a sequence of smaller steps.

How

The teacher will develop the task analysis (TA) by writing down each step necessary to complete the task/activity.

The teacher will systematically teach each step, providing assistance as needed. Over time, the prompts (assistance) are faded out, resulting in the student(s) becoming independent in this skill!

Context

Task analyses are often used to teach adaptive skills such as washing hands, tying shoes, and crossing the street. But as you can see here, they can be created for any multi-step skill! It's all about teaching clear, routine steps and fading out your support over time.

Tip

When choosing which type of prompt (assistance) to provide, consider how your students learn best! Here, this teacher is using a variety of prompts to meet the diverse needs of her students.

Write the steps

Teacher will write down the steps needed to complete the task. Each step should be one simple action.

Assist with steps: peer support

When possible, have students who have already learned the steps help others.

Assist with steps: gesture and visual

Teach each step one at a time. Here, the teacher is using a gesture and a visual to teach the step, "Walk into the library quietly."

Assist with steps: gesture

Continue providing support through each step. Here, the teacher is gesturing toward the section of books they can choose from.

Legend

⇒ Teacher preparation

Assist with the steps: model

If a student needs a little extra support, try showing them how to do the skill by doing it yourself. This is called modeling.

Reward

Some multi-step tasks have a natural reward at the end like getting to go play after tying shoes or like here, reading a book after checking it out. For other tasks, you may need to give an extra reward.

Choice Mapping

Teaching decision-making

Goal

Promote decision-making skills.

How

Use the "Choice Mapping Template" in the Tools chapter to walk through a scenario relevant to your student. Think of a situation in which they sometimes engage in expected behaviors and sometimes engage in challenging behaviors. Fill in the squares as you discuss the different pathways and their results. As described in the Building Motivation chapter, some students may need additional extrinsic motivators to help with decision-making skills. For other students, intrinsic motivators like maintaining friendships could be a sufficient reward. Here, we've illustrated a completed choice map for you as an example.

Context

This strategy should be used one-on-one with individual students, as you want to encourage their participation as much as possible. Once they've filled out their choice maps, it could be helpful to show these as a visual reminder prior to the scenarios chosen.

Tip

Engage your student in this teaching topic by allowing them to choose, draw, or write out the strategies you discuss.

Scenario

Playing basketball with friends

Safe behaviors + **Follow game rules** = **Extra computer time**

Unsafe behaviors + **Break game rules** = **No extra computer time**

Building Better Behaviors

Replacing a challenging behavior with a better behavior

Goal

Reduce challenging behaviors by teaching a more appropriate, alternative behavior.

How

Identify why a challenging behavior is occurring, and then teach the student a better, more appropriate, way to get their needs met. Recognize and reward this better behavior, and if the challenging behavior occurs, remind them what they should do instead.

Context

In a recent research study with over 100 children with developmental delays and destructive behaviors, just teaching a better behavior led to a 90% reduction in their challenging behaviors. This is the most impactful skill you can teach! Teaching this new, better behavior should happen when students are happy, relaxed, and engaged. Better behaviors often include "functional communication," meaning better ways to request wants/needs. This may include asking for help, a break, more time, space, clarification, or other expressions of self-advocacy.

Tip

It's essential that you consider how your student learns best. Try using visuals, modeling, role-play, or nearby peers to help teach this better behavior. Create many opportunities to teach and practice this skill across different situations and activities.

Understand the behavior

Take efforts to understand why the behavior occurs. See "Understanding Why Challenging Behaviors Occur" on page 64 for guidance. Here, the student often throws his materials when asked to start assignments.

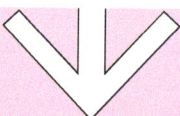

Teach a replacement behavior

Teach the student a better way to express their needs. There are many ways to teach a new behavior. You can explain it, model it, or use visuals! Here, the teacher is proactively teaching him that if he needs help or does not feel ready, he can ask for help, ask for a break, or use a self-regulation strategy.

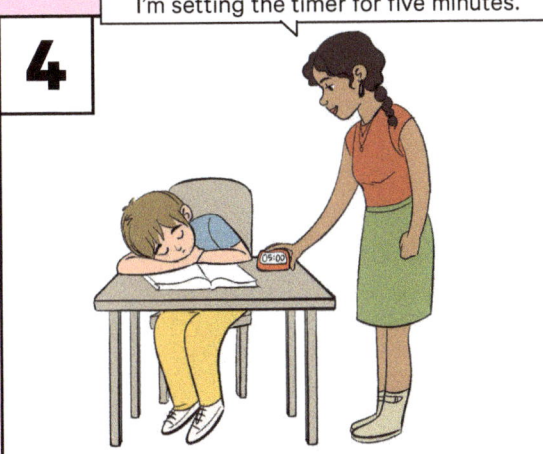

4

Range of rewards

As illustrated in the "Range of Rewards" strategy on page 118, the more independent the student is in engaging in these better behaviors, the bigger the reward should be.

Legend

 Teacher preparation
→ Student positive behavior
→ Student challenging behavior

3

Reward the better behavior

Every time the student engages in the better behavior, immediately recognize and reward this. Here, the teacher is allowing the student to take a two-minute break before beginning the assignment. If the student engages in challenging behavior, move back to step 2. Remind them of what behavior they should do.

Reward nearby peers

Recognize and reward nearby peers who are engaging in the better behavior as a way to naturally teach through peer models. This will give a hint to the student of what he should do.

Teaching to Request

Teaching how to ask for wants and needs

Goal

Reduce a challenging behavior by teaching the student to request as a better, safer way of getting their needs met.

How

First, identify why the challenging behavior is occurring. Then, as a collaborative team (preferably including a BCBA, SLP, and a teacher who knows the student best), determine what word or phrase the student should use to request their needs in these challenging moments. The SLP should guide the decision on which mode of communication is best for the student. Next, brainstorm how to create multiple opportunities to proactively teach this word or phrase across different activities and situations. Continue to proactively teach and reward when the student makes any independent attempts.

Context

While all students need to have an effective way of communicating their needs, this strategy is especially important for those who are engaging in challenging behaviors. This strategy would likely be included in their Behavior Intervention Plan (BIP).

Tip

The effectiveness of this strategy all lies in the proactive efforts to teach and collaborate! If your student has paraprofessional support, ask them to share ideas on when they can proactively teach!

1

Understand the behavior

Take efforts to first understand why the behavior occurs. Here, the student often engages in self-injurious behaviors when she needs help. See "Understanding Why Challenging Behaviors Occur" on page 64 for guidance.

4

Proactively teach

Set up situations where the student is likely to need the chosen word or phrase, and teach them in advance. Here, the teacher is demonstrating signing for "help" with the art supplies before the student attempts to open a marker cap.

Collaborate

Collaborate as a team, involving the BCBA, SLP, and the student's teacher, to select the best word or phrase for the student to use when communicating needs during challenging moments. The SLP's expertise will guide the choice of communication mode.

Plan

Brainstorm ways to create multiple opportunities for proactively teaching this word or phrase across different activities and situations.

Legend
⇒ Teacher preparation
→ Student positive behavior

Collaboratively teach

To create even more teaching moments, encourage all teachers and family members to proactively teach. Here, the paraprofessional is modeling the sign for "help" while putting together the train tracks.

Reward

Recognize and reward any attempts the student makes to request on their own.

Problem Solving

Teaching independence in finding solutions

Goal

Improve independent problem-solving skills across a variety of situations.

How

Use the "Problem Solving Template" in the Tools chapter to talk through common scenarios and guide the student through the problem-solving steps. You can ask the student to suggest the problems, or you can write down problems the student frequently encounters and randomly draw them to practice the steps. When problems occur in real life, guide the student through the steps, emphasizing their collaboration and eventual independence.

Context

Students of all ages encounter problems and would likely benefit from direct teaching of the problem-solving steps. Teachers can choose to teach problem solving as a whole-class lesson or with individual students.

Tip

When the student provides a solution suggestion (no matter how silly!), always play it out (in real life or via conversation), so they can learn on their own to determine if it was an effective solution or not.

Problem

Student encounters a problem.

Choose

Encourage the student to choose one solution and try it.

Identify

First, ask the student to identify what the problem is (even if it's obvious to you!).

Options

Guide the student in coming up with a few solution options. Validate all ideas, no matter how realistic they are.

Legend

→ Student positive behavior

→ Student may need more support

Evaluate

Determine whether the solution worked or if there's a need to try a different solution.

Conclusion

If the chosen solution solved the problem, the goal is reached. If not, return to step 4.

Self-Advocacy

Promoting voice, choice, and autonomy

Goal

Empower students to self-advocate across different situations.

How

Consider what an individual student may need to self-advocate for throughout their school day. This could relate to academics, social relationships, emotional-regulation skills, or more. Then, choose a teaching strategy to proactively teach the student how and when to request what they need to be successful. Honor and validate all attempts of self-advocacy by all students.

Context

Self-advocacy looks different across the ages, but is important for all students. Here's what it may look like in these common areas:

- Academic: Requesting accommodations, requesting for help
- Social relationships: Communicating "Leave me alone," "Stop," or expressing preferences during a social activity
- Emotional-regulation: Communicating "I need a break," "I need space," or requesting support with coping strategies

Tip

For students who are frequently bullied, try placing a visual of ways they can self-advocate in those moments inside their binder or somewhere they can easily and discreetly access.

1

Identify areas for self-advocacy

Identify the areas in which individual students may need to advocate for themselves throughout the school day, encompassing academics, social interactions, emotional-regulation, and beyond. Here, this teacher is providing the student with a list of all their accommodations they can request for.

Legend
⇒ Teacher preparation
→ Student positive behavior
→ Student may need more support

2

Create teaching opportunities

Set aside time to teach and practice how the student can self-advocate for their needs.

3

Self-advocates

When the student self-advocates, it's important that we validate and honor all of these requests to continue promoting their voice, choice, and autonomy.

Missed opportunity

There will be times when the student missed an opportunity to self-advocate. Go back to step 2 to remind them what to do. Here, all the students are packing up, and the student needs to ask for more time.

4

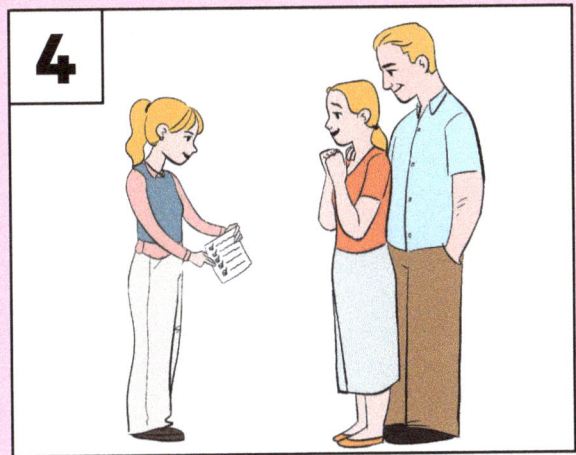

Success

By teaching students to self-advocate, we are empowering them to create their own success.

Self-Regulation

Teaching and supporting the development of coping skills

Goal

Empower students with self-regulation tools to help them navigate their days.

How

Normalizing self-regulation begins with classroom arrangement and the language we use within it. Establish a designated calm space where students can retreat as necessary, and ensure it is equipped with a range of calming visuals and materials. Proactively teach students a variety of coping strategies, recognizing that effectiveness may vary for each individual. When students face stressors, provide support in using their tools or celebrate their growing independence.

Context

Developing self-regulation skills is essential for all students and should be proactively taught starting at a young age. This is an area that may need a tiered level of support where strategies are taught and practiced classwide and additional individualized support is provided for specific students.

Tip

Teach by doing! Throughout the day, contrive scenarios where you encounter stressors and openly demonstrate to students how you use coping skills to manage challenges effectively.

Normalize self-regulation

Designate a calm corner where students can go as needed without judgment. This area should be equipped with coping skills visuals and a variety of materials to support students in regulating their emotions.

Teach self-regulation

Skills that help students self-regulate should be taught just like any other skill: proactively and with repetition.

Difficult moment, no self-regulation

When students encounter stressors throughout their day, we hope that they will use the self-regulation skills taught, but they may not.

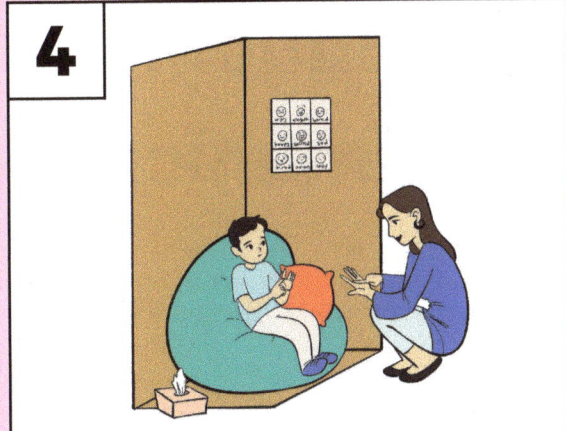

Provide support

In these moments, offer support in helping your student use some of the strategies to get back to a place of calm.

Legend
⇒ Teacher preparation
→ Student positive behavior
→ Student may need more support

Difficult moment, used self-regulation

When students encounter stressors throughout their day, we hope that they will use the self-regulation skills taught, but they may not.

Natural reward

When students effectively utilize self-regulation strategies, they can seamlessly transition back into their daily activities, experiencing the natural rewards of restored emotional stability.

Official title: Multiple exemplar training (ABA), Aided language stimulation (SLP)

Introducing Communication

Immersing students in language

Goal

Create more communication exposure.

How

Choose one core word each week (the "Word of the Week" or "WOW") to model using AAC throughout the day in a variety of contexts, teaching the full concept of that word. Aim for 100 repetitions each day! This sounds like a lot, but it is a great opportunity for collaboration across all team members.

Context

Use this strategy for new AAC learners. During this phase, you are modeling, and there is no communication expectation from them. Each week, add a new WOW, creating a cumulative language repertoire.

Tip

Speak in full sentences, but only model the WOW using AAC. For those using core boards or AAC devices, remember this as "point & say!"

Choose one core word each week to model throughout different contexts, teaching the full concept of that word. Goal: 100x per day!

Legend

- Vocal
- AAC device & Core board
- ⇒ Teacher preparation

Bold text: Core words

Standard text: Fringe words

Responding to Challenging Behaviors

Introduction

Even if we do everything we can to set our students up for success, sometimes they're going to struggle, and that's ok! That's what we're here for. It's all about knowing how to calmly and consistently respond in a supportive way. It's important for us to respond reliably so that students know what to expect from us. Approach these moments with empathy and support rather than judgment. Our reactions to students during these times can significantly influence how students respond. We can either help or cause further escalation. The way we respond makes a difference!

When taking a compassionate, trauma-informed approach to supporting students, we should always prioritize teaching new skills and rewarding positive behaviors over the use of punishment. Punishments such as time-outs, verbal reprimands, the withdrawal of privileges or points, and exclusion from activities like recess may offer temporary solutions but don't foster long-term positive behavior changes. Research advocates for a shift toward recognizing and rewarding positive behaviors, which has been shown to encourage students to repeat these behaviors. Rather than resorting to punishment, this chapter encourages transforming challenging moments into opportunities for growth and learning. Strategies such as "Tell, Show, Help" and "Pause, Redirect, Reward" focus on guiding students toward understanding what behaviors are expected of them and what skills may help in these moments.

We should be teaching our students what to do, not what not to do.

Adopting a compassionate, trauma-informed approach to supporting students places a focus on teaching new skills and recognizing positive behaviors rather than resorting to punitive measures.

Punishment vs. Not Earning a Reward

Let's consider a scenario where a student has an Individual Points Plan where they earn points for demonstrating responsible and respectful behaviors at school. Her goal is to earn ten points to receive ten minutes of computer time at the day's end as a reward. If she engages in disrespectful behavior throughout the day and falls short of the ten-point goal, a trusted staff member would review the day's events with her, indicating that the reward was not earned. The staff member should assist her with coping skills if necessary and offer encouragement for a fresh start the next day. Feeling like you missed out on earning the reward is a natural effect that makes reward systems motivating. Ideally, this experience will inspire the student to strive harder the following day to fulfill the expectations and earn the computer time reward.

In comparison, let's say that the teacher has set into the schedule that all students have ten minutes of free time on computers at the end of every day. It's built into the schedule. If a student displays disrespect toward the teacher and, consequently, the teacher decides to take away the student's computer time, that action would be considered a form of punishment. Research shows that punishment can lead to further escalation of challenging behaviors, distrust in teachers, and distrust in the reward system. Ultimately, fostering a positive learning environment built on encouragement and support rather than punitive measures is crucial for promoting student success and trust.

Avoiding vs. Preventing

When addressing challenging behaviors, it's important to distinguish between avoidance and prevention. Simply recognizing situations that pose difficulties for the student is only the first step. Yes, you could try to avoid these triggers or challenging moments; however, true prevention involves helping students develop the coping skills to navigate these situations effectively. They cannot simply avoid their triggers forever. Instead, we can better support students by proactively teaching them better, more functional skills to help them calmly and effectively manage challenging situations with confidence and resilience, empowering them to become more independent in overcoming obstacles.

Choosing a Response Strategy

In this chapter, we've illustrated step-by-step strategies for responding to challenging behaviors. When selecting the most suitable approach for your student, consider the intensity of the behavior. Whenever possible, involve the student in making decisions about how they would like to be supported in these moments.

Sometimes, people feel worried they don't know what to do when a challenging behavior occurs. The best thing you can do is stay calm and think, "How can I keep everyone safe and support them in this moment?"

No matter what type of behavior we are responding to, as teachers, it's crucial to respond to all behaviors with compassion. By identifying the triggers and establishing supportive, structured, skill-focused teaching opportunities, we lay the foundation for our approach. It is vital to incorporate trauma-informed practices that center around safety, choice, collaboration, trust, and empowerment. By embracing these principles, we create a classroom environment where students feel understood, supported, and enabled to succeed.

Responding to Low-Intensity Behaviors

Low-intensity behaviors such as verbal protest, distracting peers, or pushing work away can be frustrating for teachers, especially if these behaviors occur frequently. In this chapter, we've visualized three strategies aimed at helping you respond calmly and confidently to those low-intensity behaviors, swiftly restoring the class to an engaged learning environment.

For students who struggle with following instructions, the "Tell, Show, Help" strategy is recommended. This strategy involves gradually providing increased guidance with following directions, diminishing the necessity to repeat instructions, and minimizing frustration on both ends.

To avoid power struggles, we suggest trying the "Firm, but Flexible" strategy. While upholding firmness on essential directives like transitioning back inside or completing a test, remain flexible in your approach when students exhibit low-intensity behaviors. Offer choices within the assignment or task, allow short breaks, or explore alternative methods for students to demonstrate their understanding of the concept. Utilizing the "Firm, but Flexible Planning Template" in the Tools chapter can aid in brainstorming flexible strategies, especially when power struggles are common. If you have paraprofessionals, this would be a great activity to do together!

Turn tricky moments into teaching moments with the "Pause, Redirect, Reward" strategy. Begin by pausing the situation to regain a sense of calm. Once the student is calm, redirect them to try again using the communication, self-regulation, or executive functioning skills that you've been proactively teaching. Redirection guides students toward more appropriate behavior, offering clear alternatives. Distracting diverts their attention away from the situation temporarily without tackling the root cause. It's essential to prioritize redirection to provide students with valuable learning opportunities. Make sure to acknowledge their successful attempts at trying again, as this shows a lot of resilience!

Dr. Greg Hanley's Universal Protocols offer a structured approach to addressing precursor behaviors, which are milder behaviors that often precede more severe problem behaviors like self-injury or aggression. The core concept is to stop any instructions that may escalate the behavior to a more serious incident. By intervening early and recognizing positive behaviors, teachers can effectively prevent escalation and create a safer learning environment for all students.

Case Example

A student with a record of displaying high-intensity aggression toward both staff and peers is receiving support from his teachers. They are helping him learn self-regulation techniques and rewarding him with tokens for following classroom instructions and utilizing coping mechanisms. When he fills up his token board, he earns an iPad break.

Today, while students are expected to be working on a spelling packet, the student begins to exhibit signs of non-compliance by running around the classroom and crawling under tables. The immediate focus is on de-escalation. The teacher uses the "Pause, Redirect, Reward" strategy by giving a gentle suggestion of, "Seems like you could use a movement break! Let's step outside for a bit." While this might seem to reinforce the non-compliant behavior by allowing avoidance of work, guiding the student toward a self-regulation approach provides empathetic assistance. By allowing a brief break, we are creating an opportunity for the student to practice emotional control by not escalating further to the more severe behavior. The teacher sets a timer and when the movement break ends, she checks if the student needs to do a self-regulation strategy before returning to the expectation. Then, she reminds the student of the opportunity to earn their chosen reward: "Alright! Let's head back in, complete (xyz), and then you can enjoy your iPad break!"

Responding to High-Intensity Behaviors

When high-intensity challenging behaviors occur, it can sometimes be scary. That's a normal reaction that our mind and body respond to when experiencing an unsafe or threatening situation. Our role in these moments is to remain calm and act as a model for the student. In these situations, you and the student both need to return to a calm state before you should give any other directions.

"A dysregulated adult cannot regulate a dysregulated child."

Bruce D. Perry

If you have a student who engages in high-intensity behaviors that may cause someone harm, including aggression, self-injurious behaviors, and eloping (running away) off campus, a clear and concise support plan is needed.

These strategies would be part of the student's Behavior Intervention Plan (BIP). All staff responsible for supporting this student should have this plan memorized (See "Rethinking Behavior Intervention Plans," pg. 85). Many students who engage in this level of behavior have clear triggers and precursor behaviors. That's actually really helpful for us in knowing how to prevent the escalation of unsafe behavior proactively!

Use the "Escalation Plan Template" in the Tools chapter to outline the student's escalation cycle, which describes what their behaviors look like as they are initially agitated, as they accelerate, their peak of highest intensity behavior, and what they look like when they're de-escalating. This is a great opportunity to collaborate with your school's behavior expert and student! It's very valuable if the students can describe how they feel at each of these stages. Then, in the right column, the team collaborates to decide on appropriate responses and support strategies for each stage. Just as described above, we should prioritize responding right away to trigger and agitation behaviors in order to prevent peak behavior from occurring. In the "Escalation Plan" visual strategy, you can see how a teacher and a paraprofessional work together to implement this plan together for their student.

Within this chapter, you will find two additional visual strategies for addressing high-intensity behaviors: "Blocking Unsafe Behaviors" and "Managing Self-Injurious Behaviors." Anyone utilizing a hands-on approach to assist the student at this point should have appropriate training. After a significant behavior incident, it can be beneficial for you, the student, and any other students or staff involved to take time to rebuild rapport. This helps maintain that trusting relationship that is so important for student support.

Tell, Show, Help

Three steps to consistently follow through

Goal

Improve consistency with follow-through when giving instructions and reduce the amount of repeated instructions.

How

When giving instructions that the student has shown they can do, follow the three steps to gradually increase your support in assisting them with completing the instruction.

Context

Think about the instructions you find yourself repeating the most. That's when you should use this strategy! Remember that when you give an instruction but don't follow through, the student is learning it's okay to ignore that instruction. Be prepared to always follow through or redirect them to better requesting what they need in that moment.

Tip

Be clear and concise when giving instructions, as this enhances accessibility, reduces cognitive load, and minimizes the risk of misinterpretation.

Legend
→ Student positive behavior
→ Student challenging behavior

1 Walk quietly down the hallway, staying on the yellow line.

Tell

Give the verbal instruction and wait five seconds for the student to start.

Help

Guide the student in completing the instruction, removing your assistance whenever possible. When the instruction is completed, move on to the next instruction or activity.

Show

Give the instruction again along with a gesture (pointing) or model the task (show the student(s) how to do it). Wait five seconds for response.

Reward

As soon as the student starts the instruction, give praise. You want to recognize that they listened, but not celebrate as much as if they listened the first time you asked.

Reward

As soon as the student starts the instruction, give praise. Recognize and reward that they followed the instruction the first time you asked!

Firm, but Flexible

Firm in the instruction, flexible in how they do it

Goal

Avoid power struggles.

How

When a student engages in a low-intensity challenging behavior following an instruction, consider how you can be flexible in that moment to make that instruction easier for them, avoiding a power struggle and further escalation.

Context

Use this strategy in situations where challenging behaviors are related to following directions. It can be used with students of all ages!

Tip

Use the "Firm, but Flexible Planning Sheet" in our Tools chapter to help brainstorm what instructions are "firm" in your classroom. Then, think about ways you can offer flexibility in these moments!

Legend
⇒ Teacher preparation
→ Student positive behavior

A challenging behavior

Offer a change in location

Other Ways to be Flexible

- Adjust the pace
- Modify the expectation
- Provide choices within the task
- Offer support in completing the task
- Support with self-regulation strategies

Allow a delay in starting the task

Provide an alternative option

Pause, Redirect, Reward

Responding with support

Goal

Turn a tricky moment into a teaching moment by redirecting to a better behavior.

How

When a challenging behavior occurs, prioritize assisting the student in returning to a calm state. Pause the current situation, guide them in using a coping strategy, and once they're calm, redirect their focus to trying again, utilizing their communication, self-regulation, or self-advocacy skills. Acknowledge and reward their efforts when they demonstrate improvement in their behavior.

Context

While this strategy is beneficial for many students who engage in challenging behaviors, its effectiveness hinges on two key factors: that you have established a trusting relationship (refer to "Building Rapport") and have proactively taught replacement skills (refer to "Teaching New Skills" Chapter)

Tip

The reward given after they've "tried again" should not be as big as if they had managed the stressor on their own by using communication, self-advocacy, or self-regulation skills (See "Range of Rewards," pg. 118).

Legend
⇒ Teacher preparation
→ Student positive behavior

A Note About Extinction

When aiming to reduce challenging behaviors, you may learn of an effective strategy called extinction. To give a brief overview, extinction is when you identify why a student is engaging in a challenging behavior and then we stop responding in the way that has previously rewarded that behavior. When using this strategy, it's important to know that an extinction burst may occur. An extinction burst simply means "it may get worse before it gets better." The student is recognizing that what used to work (e.g. screaming), isn't working anymore, so they might try increasing the amount or intensity of the behavior (e.g. screaming longer, louder, or with more extreme behaviors like throwing or aggression). While this increase in challenging behaviors can seem worrisome, it's actually a sign that what you're doing is working, and it often only lasts for a very brief time.

Extinction can be a highly effective component of a behavior plan, but it's important to use it as just that—a component. We recommend prioritizing building communication skills, teaching self-advocacy, and maintaining a positive relationship with the student by supporting and validating them during challenging moments. The best approach to utilizing extinction to support your student is to use this strategy in combination with a skill-building strategy. This is the "Pause + Redirect" steps of this visualized strategy. Think of it like, "that's not how you get what you want, but here's how you can." This approach offers a more compassionate response to our students while also providing an opportunity for teaching and learning.

Challenging behavior

Although you've been proactively teaching essential skills, the student engaged in challenging behavior.

Pause

Pause by remaining calm, addressing immediate safety concerns, validating their emotions, and modeling self-regulation skills to de-escalate the situation.

Redirect

Redirect the student to try again using the strategies that you have been proactively teaching (e.g. communication, self-regulation, self-advocacy, etc.).

Reward

Once the student returns to the situation calmly and tries again using the better behavior, provide recognition for their efforts.

Blocking Unsafe Behaviors

Progressive support to maintain safety

Goal

Ensure safety for all teachers and students with the least restrictive means.

How

For any student who has a history of engaging in unsafe behaviors, it's essential that a Behavior Intervention Plan (BIP) is put in place so the team knows how to consistently and compassionately respond. We've illustrated an example of how to use least restrictive means to blocking unsafe behaviors, but this plan should be individualized for each student proactively. Follow your district's or crisis training protocol.

Context

A blocking strategy that prioritizes de-escalation and hands-off methods should be included in the individual student's BIP. It may also be beneficial to complete an Escalation Plan if the unsafe behaviors have clear triggers and precursor behaviors (lower intensity behaviors that happen first).

Tip

Work collaboratively with other nearby teachers to ensure everyone's safety. You may choose to develop secret signals or code words that give directions such as "clear the students" or "call for support" in a more discreet way.

Unsafe behavior

The student engages in an unsafe behavior such as aggression, self-injurious behavior, or running off campus.

Least restrictive

When an unsafe behavior occurs, immediately respond with one calm and clear instruction in an attempt to de-escalate the situation. Hands-off methods should be tried first. Prioritize safety by removing nearby peers or other dangerous materials.

Important Notes

- Prioritize safety by removing any objects that could be used for harm and by relocating other students if necessary.
- Remain calm and model self-regulation strategies.
- Only staff with appropriate training should engage in hands-on blocking techniques.
- Take time to rebuild rapport with the student at a later point.

Most restrictive

If behavior escalates, attempt to block and maintain safety with other hands-off methods such as creating distance or placing items between you and the student.

Only those with appropriate training should utilize hands-on methods to block unsafe behaviors as needed. Rebuilding rapport should take place later, especially if physical restraints were needed to be used.

Managing Self-Injurious Behaviors

A gentle response to repetitive, self-injurious behaviors

Goal

In the moment, decrease self-injurious behaviors by redirecting to another behavior.

How

When a self-injurious behavior occurs, immediately interrupt the behavior and redirect the student to another behavior. If you know the function of the behavior, redirect to another behavior that meets that same need. If you don't know the function yet, redirect to another behavior that will keep the student safe in that moment and will help them self-regulate.

Context

Use this strategy to respond to repetitive self-injurious behaviors such as head banging, self-biting, picking or scratching at skin, or mouthing inedible objects. This strategy is actually a punishment strategy, so while it has shown to be effective at reducing behaviors that are based in sensory needs, make sure you are also proactively teaching and rewarding replacement skills.

Tip

When choosing a replacement behavior for a sensory need, it's important to understand what about the self-injurious behavior is soothing to them. For example, in head banging, do they like the head movement feeling or is it the pressure of the contact with a hard surface? The more specific you can understand the need, the more effective your replacement behavior will be.

Self-injurious behavior

A self-injurious behavior occurs. Here, the student has left the classroom in tears and is scratching her arm, causing herself to bleed.

Interrupt

Interrupt, or block, the behavior. Use as little physical contact as possible. Teachers should have proper training if utilizing hands-on methods. Here, the teacher is providing two different squeeze balls in the attempt to interrupt the scratching behavior.

Redirect

Redirect the student to engage in a behavior that cannot be done at the same time as the self-injurious behavior. Here, the teacher and student are both squeezing the balls, which has redirected the student's hands to something more safe. You could also try redirecting to other coping skills like taking deep breaths.

Escalation Plan

A structured plan for responding to escalating behaviors

Goal

Feel confident in knowing how to consistently support a student who engages in high-intensity behaviors.

How

Meet as a team (preferably including a behavior expert and the student) to identify the student's behavior at each phase of the escalation cycle. Then, determine how the team should respond to the student at each phase. Fill in this information on our "Escalation Plan Template" found in our Tools chapter. Anyone responsible for supporting this student should have this plan memorized.

Context

Create escalation plans for students who engage in high-intensity behaviors such as aggression, self-harm, or elopement off campus. These behaviors are typically preceded by lower-intensity behaviors.

Tip

Involve the student in decision-making to hear from them how they would like to be supported at each step. Also, inform them of how the team will be responding when they are at their peak to create more predictability in our support.

A high-intensity challenging behavior

A student engages in a high-intensity challenging behavior that is commonly preceded by low-intensity behaviors.

Acceleration

When the student is starting to show signs of agitation/acceleration, make attempts to de-escalate and prepare for safety.

Create the plan

As a team, determine what the student's behavior looks like at each phase of the escalation cycle. Then, plan how staff should respond at each step.

Calm

Recognize and reward when the student is calm. Be prepared to respond to any potential triggers that could escalate them.

Legend
⇒ Teacher preparation
→ Student challenging behavior

Peak

When a student is at their peak level of escalation, the only priority here is maintaining safety. Remain calm and refrain from giving instructions.

De-escalation

When the student has shown signs that they've de-escalated, support them in self-regulation, provide comfort, and rebuild rapport as needed.

Rebuilding Rapport

Revisiting without
re-triggering

Goal

Provide opportunities for feedback and emotional
support.

How

After a high-intensity behavior, meet with the student
one-on-one once they are calm and the situation has
passed to acknowledge what occurred. Take turns
sharing how the incident affected everyone. Discuss
possible triggers and solutions. Rebuild trust by
showing empathy and respect.

Context

This strategy benefits both students and staff,
particularly if the experience involved a restrictive
practice or high-intensity behavior with potential
traumatic impacts.

Tip

If another peer was involved in the incident, guide
both students through the process with sensitivity and
empathy, encouraging open communication and mutual
understanding.

A challenging behavior

Although you've been proactively teaching essential
skills, the student engaged in challenging behavior.

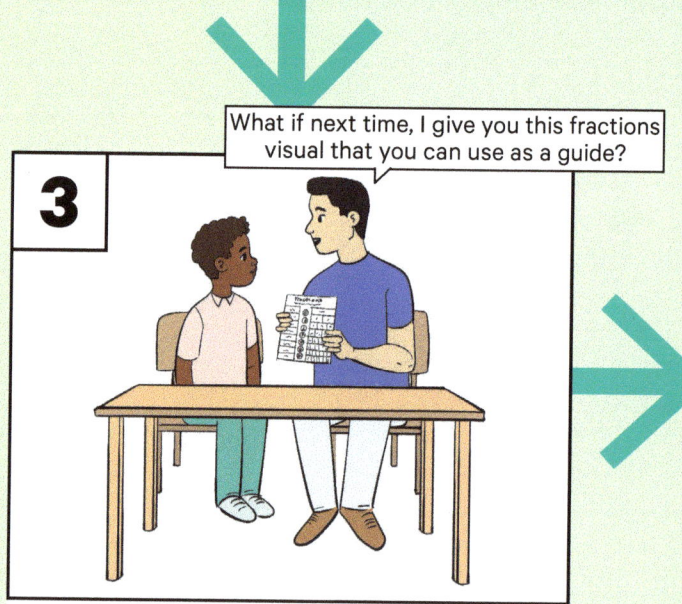

Reflect

Together with the student, reflect on what
may have caused the behavior and problem-
solve ways to better support or manage this
trigger in the future.

Meet with the student

When the student is calm and the situation has passed (either later in the day or the following day), meet with the student one-on-one to acknowledge what occurred.

Discuss the impact

In a calm, nonjudgmental way, share how the incident impacted you or others, and encourage the student to do the same.

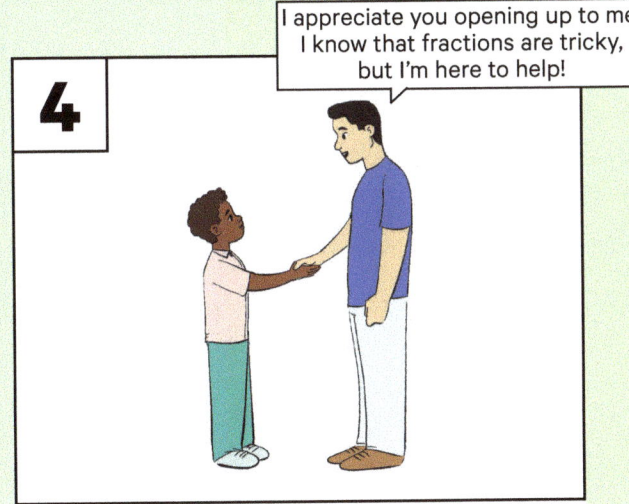

Reconnect

Re-establish trust by showing empathy toward the student's perspective and ensuring you can both move forward.

Reflection Questions

- Who was involved in the incident or immediately prior?
- What happened?
- Where did it happen?
- Why did it happen?
- What did we learn?

Legend
⇒ Teacher preparation
→ Student positive behavior

Templates & Tools

Introduction

To assist you in using the strategies taught in this book in your classroom, we have created a collection of custom-made visual templates and tools. You can access this full collection by scanning the QR code below. You can also email us at info@abavisualized.com and we would be happy to send them to you that way. We hope that these provide you, your classroom staff, and the IEP team with the resources and support necessary to ensure your students' success in reaching their academic and behavioral goals. We have included instructions on utilizing the visuals, templates, and tools in the scenarios where they can be most beneficial. You have our permission to make copies of them to share with your team; we just kindly request that you acknowledge *Behavior Essentials, Visualized*. Thank you!

Or go to
https://shorturl.at/brAJ1

The Benefits of Visual Supports

Visual supports, which utilize images or text instead of spoken words, serve as a powerful tool for communication. They effectively convey information in ways that are accessible to students with language delays. However, they are not just helpful for students with language delays! We all use similar kinds of visual supports in our day-to-day lives because, sometimes, a visual representation of information is the best way for us to process information. In our daily routines, we often turn to various visual aids as they serve as effective tools for processing information. Street signs guide our way, calendars help us manage our schedules, and grocery lists ensure we get what we need. These visual cues play a crucial role in supporting our daily tasks.

Visual supports are invaluable for students to acquire new skills, understand expectations, and enhance self-management abilities. By utilizing visuals, teachers can effectively convey information to students, facilitating improved communication and understanding. Consistent use of visual supports fosters independence and can diminish challenging behaviors.

Research indicates that visual supports help by:

- Enabling students to concentrate on key terms and ideas
- Transforming abstract concepts into clear visual representations
- Encouraging students to express their thoughts more easily
- Establishing routine and structure
- Reducing anxiety and frustration
- Facilitating smooth transitions
- Enhancing understanding
- Decreasing challenging behaviors

Some neurodiverse students may find it difficult to understand and follow instructions that are only provided vocally. Visuals make instructions last longer than spoken words alone. Visuals can also help teachers communicate what they expect and allow students to express their thoughts and needs more effectively. This decreases frustration and may help reduce challenging behaviors that result from difficulty communicating.

For students who experience anxiety relating to changes in routines or when they are in unfamiliar situations, visuals can help them understand what to expect and what will happen next in order to reduce anxiety.

The use of visuals in the classroom can improve classroom behaviors and enhance learning for students. We encourage you to explore our collection of tools and templates and see how incorporating visuals can enhance your teaching methods and promote student success.

Within this collection, we offer visuals that you can use directly with your students like our "Greetings at the Door Poster," "Token Boards," "Class Pass Tickets," and "Behavior Contract." Additionally, there are visuals designed to aid teachers in planning, organizing, and tracking progress effectively.

References

Aupperle, R., Aupperle, L., Madurski, L., & Madurski, A. (2012). Utilizing pre-service teacher preparation programs to increase the number of fully qualified special education teachers. Educational Leadership Review of Doctoral Research, 1(1), 3-14.

Autism Little Learners Podcast. (2024). Executive Functioning Skills for Autistic Preschoolers.
American Psychiatric Association. (2013). Diagnostic and Statistical Manual of Mental Disorders (5th ed.). Washington, DC.

Bacotti, J.K., Peters, K.P. & Vollmer, T.R. (2022). Parents Are People Too: Implementing Empirically Based Strategies During Daily Interactions. Behav Analysis Practice, 15, 986–1000.
Baker, Jed. (2008). No More Meltdowns: Positive Strategies for Managing and Preventing Out-of-Control Behavior. Arlington, TX: Future Horizons, Inc.

Baker, P. A. (2017). Attending to debriefing as post-incident support of care staff in intellectual disability challenging behaviour services: An exploratory study. International Journal of Positive Behavioural Support, 7(1), 38-44.

Blodgett, C., & Dorado, J. (2016). A selected review of trauma-informed school practice and alignment with educational practice. California Endowment: San Francisco, CA.

Boutot, A., & Hume, K. (2012). Beyond time out and table time: Today's Applied Behavior Analysis for learners with autism. Education and Training in Autism and Developmental Disabilities, 47, 23-38.

Boesch, M.C., Taber-Doughty, T., Wendt, O., & Smalts, S.S. (2015). Using a behavioral approach to decrease self-injurious behavior in an adolescent with severe autism: a case study. Education and Treatment of Children, 38(3), 305-328.

Bisson, J., & Andrew, M. (2005). Psychological treatment of post-traumatic stress disorder (PTSD) Jonathan Bisson, ed. Cochrane Database of Systematic Reviews.

Carr, E.G., & Durand, V.M. (1985). Reducing problem behaviors through functional communication training. Journal of Applied Behavior Analysis, 18(2), 111-126.

Chafouleas, S. M., Johnson, J. H., Overstreet, S., & Santos, N. M. (2016). Toward a blueprint for trauma-informed service delivery in schools. School Mental Health, 8, 144–162.

Chasing the Intact Mind: How the Severely Autistic and Intellectually Disabled Were Excluded from the Debates That Affect Them Most by Amy S. F. Lutz

Cohen, J. A., Mannarino, A. P., & Deblinger, E. (2016). Treating trauma and traumatic grief in children and adolescents. Guilford Publications.

Cook, J. R., DeLuca, N. L., Bergman, P. S., Koenig, K. P., Kirby, A. V., & Jawad, A. F. (2002). Traumatic events in the lives of individuals with disabilities. Journal of Rehabilitation, 68(4), 4-13.

Cooper, J.O., Heron, T.E., & Heward, W.L. (2019). Applied behavior analysis (3rd ed.). Upper Saddle River, NJ: Pearson Education, Inc.

Critchfield, T.S., Doepke K.J., Epting, K.L., Becirevic, A., Reed, D.D., Fienup, D.M., Kremsreiter, J.L., Ecott, C.L. (2017). Normative Emotional Responses to Behavior Analysis Jargon or How Not to Use Words to Win Friends and Influence People. Behav Anal Pract, 10(2), 97-106.

De Bruin, C., Deppeler, J., Moore, D., & Diamond, N. (2013). Public School-Based Interventions for Adolescents and Young Adults With an Autism Spectrum Disorder: A Meta-Analysis. Review of Educational Research, 83(4), 521-550.

Durand, V.M., & Carr, E.G. (1991). Functional communication training to reduce challenging behavior: maintenance and application in new settings. Journal of Applied Behavior Analysis, 24(2), 251-264.

Durand, V.M., & Moskowitz, L. (2015). Functional communication training: thirty years of treating challenging behavior. Topics in Early Childhood Special Education, 35(20), 116-126.

Eckenrode, L., Fennell, P., & Hearsey, K. (2004). Tasks Galore for the Real World. Raleigh, NC: Tasks Galore.

Eldevik, S., Hastings, R.P., Hughes, J.C., Jahr, E., Eikeseth, S., & Cross, S. (2009). Meta-analysis of early intensive behavioral intervention for children with autism. Journal of Clinical Child & Adolescent Psychology.

Eredics, N. (2018). Inclusion in Action: Practical Strategies to Modify Your Curriculum. Brookes Publishing.

Ervin, S. (2022). The Classroom Behavior Manual: How to Build Relationships with Students, Share Control, and Teach Positive Behaviors.

Falcomata, T.S., Muething, C.S., Gainey, S., Ho man, K., & Fragale, C. (2013). Further evaluations of functional communication training and chained schedules of reinforcement to treat multiple functions of challenging behavior. Behavior Modification, 37(6), 723-746.

Gerhardt, P.F., Weiss, M.J., & Delmolino, L. (2004). Treatment of severe aggression in an adolescent with autism: non-contingent reinforcement and functional communication training. The Behavior Analyst Today, 4(4), 386-394.

Gioia, G. A., Isquith, P. K., Retzlaff, P. D., & Espy, K. A. (2002). Confirmatory factor analysis of the behavior rating inventory of executive function (BRIEF) in a clinical sample. Child Neuropsychology, 8(4), 249.

Hall, S., & Oliver, C. (1992). Differential effects of severe self-injurious behaviour on the behaviour of others. Behavioural Psychotherapy, 20, 355-366.

Hanley, G. (2021). A Perspective on Today's ABA by Dr. Greg Hanley. Retrieved from https://practicalfunctionalassessment.com/2021/09/09/a-perspective-on-todays-aba-by-dr-greg-hanley/

Harvey, Shane T et al. (2009). Updating a Meta-Analysis of Intervention Research with Challenging Behaviour: Treatment Validity and Standards of Practice. Journal of Intellectual & Developmental Disability, 34(1), 67–80.

Hart Barnett, J. (2018). Three Evidence-Based Strategies that Support Social Skills and Play Among Young Children with Autism.

Hastings, R.P. (2010). Staff in special education settings and behavior problems: Towards a framework for research and practice. Educational Psychology, 25(2-3), 207-221.

Hastings, R.P. (2010). Support staff working in intellectual disability services: The importance of relationships and positive experiences. Journal of Intellectual and Developmental Disability, 35(3), 207-210.

Jennings, P. A. (2018). The trauma-sensitive classroom: Building resilience with compassionate teaching. New York: W.W. Norton & Company.

Kentucky Department of Education. (2021). Trauma-Informed Discipline Response and Behavior System.

Mathur, S. K., Renz, E., & Tarbox, J. (2024). Affirming neurodiversity within applied behavior analysis. Behavior Analysis in Practice.

Minahan, J. (2014). The behavior code companion: Strategies, tools, and interventions for supporting students with anxiety-related or oppositional behaviors. Cambridge, MA: Harvard Education Press.

Minahan, J. (2019). Building positive relationships with students struggling with mental health. Phi Delta Kappan, 100(6), 56–59.

Minahan, J., & Rappaport, N. (2012). The behavior code: A practical guide to understanding and teaching the most challenging students. Cambridge, MA: Harvard Education Press.

National Child Traumatic Stress Network, Schools Committee. (2017). Creating, supporting, and sustaining trauma-informed schools: A system framework. Los Angeles, CA, and Durham, NC: National Center for Child Traumatic Stress.

National Council on Teacher Quality. (2014). Encouraging more high school students to consider teaching.

Pokrivčáková, S., et al. (2015). Teaching Foreign Languages to Learners with Special Educational Needs: e-textbook for foreign language teachers (pp. 83-90). Nitra: Constantine the Philosopher University.

Substance Abuse and Mental Health Services Administration. (2014). SAMHSA'S Concept of Trauma and Guidance for a Trauma-Informed Approach. SAMHSA's Trauma and Justice Strategic Initiative.

Sulkowski, M. L., & Michael, K. (2014). Meeting the mental health needs of homeless students in schools: A Multi-Tiered System of Support framework. Children and Youth Services Review, 44, 145-151.

Tarbox, C., Tarbox, J., Bermudez, T.L. et al. (2023). Kind Extinction: A Procedural Variation on Traditional Extinction. Behavior Analysis in Practice.

Taylor, B. A., LeBlanc, L. A., & Nosik, M. R. (2019). Compassionate Care in Behavior Analytic Treatment: Can Outcomes be Enhanced by Attending to Relationships with Caregivers? Behavior Analysis in Practice, 12(3), 654-666.

Terrasi, S., & de Galarce, P. C. (2017). Trauma and learning in America's classrooms. Phi Delta Kappan, 98(6), 35–41.